Traditional Institutions of Meghalaya

A Study of *Doloi* and his Administration

Dr. L.S. Gassah
Professor and Head
Department of Political Science
North-Eastern Hill University
Shillong

2024
Regency Publications
A Division of
Astral International Pvt. Ltd.
New Delhi – 110 002

First Published, 1998
Reprinted, 2024

ISBN 978-81-86030-49-3 (HB)

Published by : **Regency Publications**
A Division of
Astral International Pvt. Ltd.
– ISO 9001:2015 Certified Company –
4736/23, Ansari Road, Darya Ganj
New Delhi-110 002
Ph. 011-43549197, 23278134
E-mail: info@astralint.com
Website: www.astralint.com

Printed at : **Replika Press Pvt Ltd**

Preface

This book *Traditional Institutions of Meghalaya — A Case Study of Doloi and His Administration*, is the result of my long experience in research and teaching on the subject of Government and Politics in North East India. While reading desultorily through whatever materials available on such important topics like the traditional socio-political institutions of the different tribes of North East India, I found it very difficult at the initial stage to have a comprehensive idea about these institutions because the materials are so scattered in different books and journals. This makes one's reading difficult. Obviously, this subject will be more difficult for the students who are interested in this field of study. The main reason for this is because of the scattered materials and the absence, in most of the case, of any systematic treatment of the subject matter we are striving for at the moment.

The short opening remarks made above, are generally true in respect of most of the tribes in North East India. Coming nearer to our own State, Meghalaya, the picture is not much different from others. There is no denying the fact as far as the traditional socio-political institutions are concerned, few books have been written (and more such books are perhaps in the pipeline) on all the three major tribes of Meghalaya — the Khasis, the Jaintias and the Garos. Most of these books are general in character, dealing mostly on the history and culture of the people as well as on an important milestone in the history of the people in their relationship with the British. Of late, there are a good number of research articles published in various journals, proceedings of research organisations in the region, souvenirs and newspapers. Therefore all such articles are all scattered everywhere. Another important sources of information are to be found in most of the old archival records and reports written by the British officials stationed and serving in these areas. Such sources of information have been retrieved by few research scholars which may be lying at their own personal files and library. Unless these personal collections are published publicly, either in the form of books or research articles, I am afraid, they may not see the light of the day. The general public and especially the students may not even know the existence of such sources of information if they are kept hidden somewhere for private consumption only. However, I am personally very glad to see that most of these hidden treasures have already been put to light in the form of printed materials. But still, I once again want to drive home a point which I raised earlier that these printed materials are all scattered everywhere. It is therefore high time that the public readers in general, and the students in particular, must have these written materials in their hands, prepared by serious researchers in a systematic form and with a knowledge of scientific methodology.

Against this background, this book tries first of all to put things as far as practical in a systematic manner. Secondly, most of these materials wherever and whenever we have been able to lay our hands on are put together to make it a little bit easier for the readers. As this book is primarily meant for the students, it is therefore our purpose to collect most of those scattered materials so that in case one finds it difficult and time consuming to search all that have come into their knowledge about that has been written but could not lay their hands on them, this small attempt may therefore help in that sense. This is of course, a trial and error attempt. We are therefore open to constructive suggestions for better improvement in the future. We do not also claim any perfection in a humble attempt like this one.

The Jaintia society is a society in transition. In between this transitional period, we cannot deny the fact that the society still keeps its tradition, its traditional social and political institutions, its culture and usages and such other varied institutions that existed since time immemorial. Even the mighty British administration could not but retain some of the fine traditional institutions of the Jaintias. They had of course, abolished the office of the Jaintia *Syiem* since the 15th of March 1835, but had to retain the offices of the other traditional institutions like for example, the *Doloi*, *Pator* and *Waheh Chnong*, and these were allowed to continue functioning right through the British period and of course even today. But, in between this long transitional period, many changes had taken place and change is still to be seen even today under a new type of administrative set up coupled with parliamentary democracy.

Keeping the broad spectrum in mind, we have therefore attempted to analyse the situation as it existed in the past and as it is today to see how tradition, continuity and change have worked in the Jaintia society which has experienced a number of changes throughout the long period of its history.

Deptt. of Political Science
North-Eastern Hill University
Shillong

L.S. Gassah

Contents

Introduction

The institution of chiefship among the hill tribes of North-East India is a common feature. This institution prevailed and is still prevailing among many of the tribal communities of the region. Though some tribes have abolished the office of their chief, we still find the existence of the same among majority of them. For example, among the Mizos, the office of the once powerful *Lal* or chief had been abolished under the Assam — Lushai Hills District (Acquisition of Chiefs' Rights) Act of 1955 with a provision to pay compensation to the chiefs. Among the Jaintias, the office of *Syiem* (King or Raja) was abolished by the British in 1835 after the Jaintia Hills was placed under the British administration. However, the British retained the other offices of the traditional chiefs in the area, like the *Doloi, Pator* and *Waheh Chnong* (village headman) to assist the British authorities in running the administration of the area concerned.

On the basis of the powers and functions held by the chiefs of numerous tribes of the region, they can be classified into different categories depending upon the extent of power entrusted or held by them. Further, the customary law of succession and the methods of election or selection also differ from tribe to tribe and area to area. Variation in the laws of succession to the office could be found even within the same tribal community. The laws of succession also determined the amount of power entrusted to the chief either by the chief's family or clan or the council of elders or the villagers themselves or whichever body responsible in determining the succession process. A chief is either elected or selected for a definite period or for a life time.

Among the tribes which follow the patrilineal system and where chiefship has become hereditary, the law of primogeniture is generally observed. At the same time, it is a practice that the eldest surviving male child of the previous or deceased chief may not inherit the office if he is known to be incapable, cowardly or having positive drawbacks. From this it is thus evident that the son becomes the chief by virtue of his personal qualifications. Among some other tribes or communities, a chief is elected to the office on the basis of his personal ability or qualifications rather than on the ground of hereditary rights, or still among other tribes, the office is strictly confined to the members of the privileged original or founding clan or clans. These clans are regarded as such because it were they who were the first or earliest settlers in a village. Even those chiefs who inherited their office on hereditary basis, the question of inheritance depends whether the society adopts a matrilineal or patrilineal system. In some cases, the principle of hereditary cheiftainship was introduced by the British. This they did in order to ensure political stability and loyalty of the chiefs towards the British government. Basically, not a single typology of chiefship could be found to exist among the various tribes of the North-Eastern region.

Different chiefs functioned differently. The powers and functions of the chiefs differ from one tribe to another. Some chiefs function despotically and thus become the vehicle or agent of oppression and suppression over their subjects; others run the administration under their respective jurisdiction in a democratic manner. Basically, the powers and functions of a chief depend on the customary laws of inheritance governing the office or the methods of election or selection. As stated earlier, some chiefs were despotic and autocratic rulers who wielded much power over their people or subjects. Under such a circumstance, all powers and functions are concentrated in their hands. In this case, their words become the law of the land.

Among a larger number of tribes, a chief plays a dual role being both the secular and religious head of the village. The chief in that case has two sets of functions — secular and religious. Among some tribal communities in the region, the latter functions have to be performed by the chief inspite of the existence of the village priest or in consultation with such a religious functionary. The secular duties and functions of a chief are manifold and far outnumber and outweigh his religious and ceremonial functions. Further, negligence of the secular duties and functions may cost the chief his office. In fact, among many tribes whenever a chief has been compelled to forfeit or lay down his office, it was due to his inability to discharge the secular and administrative functions satisfactorily. Thus, negligence to properly discharging secular duties and functions is a very serious matter concerning the chief. Secular duties and functions entrusted to the chief are multifarious; they actually include the whole gamut of administration. Besides this, a chief has also emergency powers and war-time duties to perform in times of war or during other serious crises that may befall upon the people. He plays the role of a commander-in-chief of his warriors on the battle front. Indeed, in those old days when wars were the order of the day, the chief physical prowess and strength were in great demand than his sagacity or other qualities of head and heart, though no doubt these are also equally important.

A chief powers and functions also include judicial matters. A chief is not only the administrative head of the village but he is also the fountain of justice. He therefore acts as a judge and decides disputes among the villagers and clans. However, among some tribal communities of the region, the chief alone cannot perform the administration of justice. In this case, therefore, a chief acts only as a judge and the *Durbar* or council performs the duty of a jury. In this way it is the joint venture of the two traditional institutions while deciding or performing judicial functions. The chief has therefore to consult the council members or elders for administering justice. Both the chief and the councillors had to sit together in hearing and settling the cases brought before them. They together will dispense, judge and administer justice. The chief cannot ignore the part and function played by the *Durbar* or council of elders in the areas where they have been vested with judicial powers. Along with the chief, the council of elders therefore constituted a court. Such a court becomes the highest court of justice within the jurisdiction of the chief and decides all types of cases and disputes according to the customary laws of the society. A chief and the other traditional institutions played an important role in the administration of justice.

Among those tribes whose chief is elected by the people, his powers and functions are circumscribed by them or by the different councils set up by the people themselves. Such chief has to run the administration according to the traditions, customs, usages and culture of the tribes or community concerned. In many areas of decision-making process, the general will of the people has always to be taken into consideration as the people and not the chief in such a situation enjoy the highest power and thus become the final authority. In this case, the people elected or selected their chief in order to supervise the administration and look after the people pertaining to their welfare and not to supress or oppress them. Should the chief show any symptom of misbehaviour against his people, they, on their part, have the power and authority to strip him of his office.

In some areas, the chief is always assisted in his administration by a village council or a council of elders or village headmen or the heads of different clans residing in the village. Where such an arrangement existed, there is always a joint venture or cooperation to run the administration smoothly for the general well-being of all the inhabitants. These different types of councils play an important role in the traditional polity. Wherever such councils are in existence, it is the bounden duty of the chief to consult the council members by convening periodic sessions. Matters concerning the clan and village affairs are to be discussed thoroughly and unanimous decisions are to be taken before their finalisation. In this respect, the chief cannot ignore the powers and functions enjoyed and entrusted on these councils. Mini-parliament at the grass-root level could therefore be said to have worked among such people.

The rights and privileges enjoyed by a chief differ from tribe to tribe. It also depends upon the powers and functions of a chief. A powerful and despotic chief can exert pressure and demand numerous types of payments to be made by his subjects. Such a chief can claim as his rights and privileges almost everything in the village. He can claim the entire village as his own, its lands, forests, their produces and everything that grows and lives there. The people have even to pay annually certain amount of paddy after the harvest, certain portions of the animals killed by them, honey and salt collected by them and such other things to the chief. Moreover, the chief is also allotted the best plot of land for cultivation. He has the right to be the first person to choose a plot of land for himself before any others. Even the cultivation of his land is done by the people without payment of labour cost. Among the Mizos, the chief (Lal) however used to offer feast or *zu* (rice beer) to the people after the completion of the work. Failure to contribute or pay fines or taxes imposed by the chief will eventually lead to different kinds of punishments. A clear example of such rights and privileges enjoyed by a chief could be found to have existed specially among the Mizos and Nagas. Among other tribes a chief does not enjoy such enormous rights and privileges as among the Mizos and Nagas. Such rights and privileges if any, are confined to few things only. For example, among the Khasis, Jaintias and Garos these privileges are confined to certain plots of land, fines imposed by the chief and tolls from the markets under the control of a chief.

This is only a brief introductory remark on the institution of chiefship in the pre-British period. Many changes had taken place after the British either annexed or took over the administration of the hill areas of North-East India.

The British administration had tremendous effects on the traditional institutions in general and the powers and functions of the chiefs in particular among the various tribes of North-East India. These effects were in different forms and extent of magnitude because the British did not adopt a single or uniform approach or policy towards the different tribes of the region. With regard to their policy towards the traditional chiefs of the different areas, the British were very particular to see that such indigenous institutions be made useful tools in their hands for the furtherance of their imperialistic interests in such a difficult hilly terrain and expensive area as far as administration was concerned. The British therefore allowed this indigenous system of administration through the chiefs to continue, because they wanted to rule the turbulent tribes of this most difficult terrain with minimum expenditure. In order to partly overcome this problem, the British made the chiefs as their allies, because rational imposition of colonial administration became easier only through the control of the chiefs first and then the same was made in turn to control the mass. This provided the colonial rulers a short-cut way to ultimately control the people without taking any direct mass line of action that would have been a more hazardous process and more expensive financially. In this process, the British recognised only the office of the chief and not the people in dealing with the tribal administration. Due to such an approach undertaken by the British, among some tribal communities, the chief became more powerful and more authoritarian towards their people than before the coming of the British because their actions were now backed by the colonial rulers after they took over the administration of the tribal areas.

In the changed circumstances, the British appointed the chiefs not only to assist them in running the administration but also used them as 'commission agents' to collect and extract taxes and such other payments from their own people and deposited the same to the British treasury. This helped the British to raise their income and revenue even from the hitherto difficult hilly terrain of the region. Accordingly, due to the services rendered by the chiefs in the collection of taxes, they received certain percentage of remuneration out of the total revenue collection. The traditional chiefs in this way became the tools in the hands of the colonial rulers who took the maximum political advantage after giving them a sense of political safety and stability by their policy of official settlement.

The other notable effect of the British administration on the traditional institutions of chieftainship was the deviation it made from the customary practices of appointment of chiefs. The new structural variability introduced by the British was to draw and appoint the chiefs even from among the commoners, a practice foreign to the local people. For example, during the British rule over the then Lushai Hills, under their astute administrative acumen, they started increasing the number of chiefs drawing them from among the commoners other than the chief's clans and allotting them vacant lands for the establishment of their villages. This was also done as a reward for the services rendered by many such commoners' clans during the Anglo-Lushai wars. The British tactfully did this in order to ensure loyalty and stability towards their administration among such turbulent tribal people. The British were responsible in creating a totally new set of traditional leadership contrary to the customary tradition of the local people.

Since India's Independence, the powers of the traditional chiefs had been threatened by the new administrative set up especially due to the introduction of the District Council under the Sixth Schedule to the Constitution, since 1952. The District Council has a tremendous effect on the powers and functions of the traditional institutions and chiefship in the hill areas of North-East India where such a Council was introduced. The introduction of the Sixth Schedule did not bring improvement in the power and functions or the status and position of the traditional chiefs. On the contrary, the new power structure has radically reduced the powers of the Chiefs. Moreover, on many occasions, there have been tussles between the traditional elite represented by the chiefs and headmen and the modern political elite of popular elected representatives. On one pretext or another, the chiefs or headmen might be suspended or even dismissed by the District Council on charges like insubordination and malpractices. The tussle is still a continuing affair.

The traditional chiefs are now treated by the District Council as its subordinate officials. They are completely under the District Council's control. For example, in the case of Meghalaya, under the provision of paragraph 3(i)(g) of the Sixth Schedule, the District Council has been empowered to make laws with respect to — 'the Appointment and Succession of Chiefs and Headmen'. The United Khasi-Jaintia Hills Autonomous District Council (Appointment and Succession of Chiefs and Headmen) Act, 1959, made law not only for its authority to appoint the Chiefs and Headmen, but also the removal and suspension of the same by the Executive Committee of the District Council if in its opinion these incumbents violated the terms and conditions of their appointment. At a particular point of time, the United Khasi-Jaintia Hills Autonomous District Council even suggested to the State Government not to correspond with the traditional chiefs directly. This created much resentment between the two authorities. The relationship between the two was and is still all along under strains.

CHAPTER I

Doloi: Processes of the Evolution of the Office

The office of *Doloi* in Jaintia Hills did not come into existence all of a sudden. Different processes of traditional polity formation gradually took place at different period of time before such an important institution was created by the society concerned. Other traditional institutions were at work among the Jaintia people right from the family and clan and at the village level of administration. Having found that these institutions at the grass-root level could not properly deliver the goods on account of their limitations and due to the increase of population and size of the territory coupled with the ever increasing number of functions to be performed, the Jaintia people in their wisdom decided to create an institution above that of the family, clan and village. Such a higher institution of a political unit would cater to the needs and bring together the different groups of families and clans and villages under one central authority. This process took place when the groups of migrants to the present Jaintia Hills came to lead a more settled way of life. After permanently settled in the land, further development in the organisation of their traditional polity also took place. There were few wars to fight and thus different groups of migrants in order to make themselves more secure from future aggressions, groups of villages with their clan clusters joined together to form a *Raid*, which may also be called a semi-State. With the formation of the *Raid*, people were no longer nomads outside their *Raid*, though they continued to move from place to place within their own *Raid*. Thus, the Jaintias were then semi-nomadic when the *Raid* was formed. They did not frequently move outside their *Raid* for fear of losing their political rights in another *Raid*.[1]

The Jaintia people were one of the first few migrants to have come and occupied their present habitat. Moreover, during the migratory period, they came in different groups or batches. Each of these batches had their own leader or chief who also played the role of a religious functionary. The different batches after they finally came to the present Jaintia Hills, decided to settle here permanently and stop advancing any further. There may be many factors responsible for taking such a decision. Perhaps during their migration while moving from place to place either in search of shelter from their enemies invasion or in search of better suitable lands for cultivation, they found the present hills to be a safer place from the point of view of its strategic position as far as their enemies are concerned. Comparatively, they also found their present habitat to be more fertile and suitable for cultivation than the other places which they came across on their way. Their settled life led to the increasing number of other batches who joined later on to settle together in this place.

During the migratory period of the people, a sort of leadership had emerged. Any senior male member of the family or clan or any male member, generally a priest, considered to having divine knowledge would become the natural leader. Since the decision to migrate in some cases required an immediate attention, a leader in such a migratory society was a very powerful one and could not be a democratic leader.[2] It may further be noted that during such migratory period, each batch was under the concentrated power of the sacred chief, the priest (*U Langdoh*) who used to be the mediator between the people and their God, the Creator (*U Tre Kirot*).[3]

Thus we find that at the earliest period of time, the Jaintia people were under the administration and leadership of *U Langdoh,* both at the village and groups of villages or *Raid* levels. The *Langdoh* combined in himself both the sacred and secular functions. The first incumbent of the office of the priest of the *Raid* was elected from among the priestly families of the villages of the *Raid*.[4] But with the increase in the number of families and clans, area and size of population, there was also an increase in the number of duties and functions to be performed single-handedly by the *Langdoh*.[5] The Jaintia people in their wisdom felt the need that the administrative set up should be re-structured. As a result, it was necessary to bifurcate the dual functions of sacred or religious and secular affairs which were under the concentrated power and authority of the *Langdoh*. In the process, it was decided to hand over those functions which were purely sacred or religious in nature to the priest and the other functions which were purely administrative or secular to the secular chief, *U Doloi* (Provincial Governor). Thus, the office of the *Doloi* came into existence.

U Doloi is therefore the chief of the next higher political unit called *Ka Elaka* or Province, which was formed by combining a group of villages or *Raids*. For example, the Jowai *Elaka* was formed by combining the four *Raids*, that of Chyrmang, Jowai, Tuber and Yalong. But in the subsequent development, there were other processes too, which were responsible for the creation of more *Elakas* in Jaintia Hills. Occasionally, an extra tier between the *Elaka* and the village was instituted wherever the *Elaka* was too large to be managed by one *Doloi*. Such an extra tier was usually placed under a Lieutenant-Governor or *U Pator*. A *Doloi* could either function directly or through his deputy, *U Pator* with the assistance of *Ki Tymmen Ki San* or simply *Ki Wasan* (Elders) who are the representatives of their respective clans.[6] Once a *Doloi* takes up his office, he normally holds it for the rest of his life. But he may be punished, expelled or stripped of his office, should he arouse sufficient hostility to his people. The people hold the highest authority; they elect their chiefs for the purpose of supervising the administration and do not allow and tolerate the chiefs who behave in a despotic manner which may eventually lead to oppression or suppression of the people. The powers and functions of the *Dolois* are therefore circumscribed by the society which differentiate them from other chiefs prevailing among other tribal communities of the region.

It will not be out of place to mention here that in the sociopolitical life of the Jaintia people, the smallest social unit is the family. The families and clans naturally formed the smallest unit of the political society called *Chnong* or a village. Centering around families and clans was generally a society where leadership fell on the seniormost male member called *U Knyi*, literally a maternal uncle of the family or clan. This was a natural way for the Jaintia families and clans to adopt while migrating from place to place. Interestingly enough, there were traditions where the seniormost male member could be an infant of one day old in case where adult male members were either killed in fighting against the enemies or when an older person had an unclean record. This tradition holds good till today in most religious functions in certain families having no adult male elders or having older male members with doubtful records. In case where there was no male relative at all, the family and clan concerned had to hire a male member to be a religious leader. In such a situation, the Jaintias called it *Thied Knyi* which means literally to purchase a maternal uncle.[7] The resort to purchase someone from outside the family or clan to act or play the role of an uncle might sound quite unusual or even strange to those who do not know much about the inner Jaintia society. But this was actually practised by certain families or clans in case the need arises. The resort to such a practice is not unusual or strange if we are to assess and understand the role played by the maternal uncle both in the secular and religious functions.

Subsequent upon the increase in the number of families and clans as well as population and territory, ultimately led to the setting up of a village. This obviously gave rise to the increase in the number of functions to be performed single-handedly by the uncle of the family or clan. The family or clan uncle under these circumstances found it very difficult to look after the multifarious affairs all by himself. The people therefore felt the need of centralisation of all those functions in the hands of one person or authority but at a higher level than that of the family and clan to supervise the administration. In the process, the office of the *Waheh Chnong* or village Headman came into existence.

Before the British annexation of Jaintia Hills took place, the Jaintias had a three-tier system of administration. Under such a set up, the office of the *Syiem* or King occupied the apex position in the hierarchy; in the middle or zonal level, there were and still the *Dolois* or Provincial Governors in each *Elaka*, and the office of the *Waheh Chnong* or village Headman stands at the lowest rung in the ladder of administration. Occasionally an extra tier also exists under the *Pator* or Lieutenant-Governor. The office of the Jaintia *Syiem* was abolished by the British and lapsed in 1835 after the annexation and possession of the land by the latter. The British authority therefore declared the whole of Jaintia Hills along with few other villages in Khasi Hills as

British Areas. Though the British authority completely abolished the office of the *Syiem*, on the other hand, they retained and allowed the offices of *Doloi*, *Pator*, and village Headman to continue. These offices also continue till today aiding and assisting the District Council in the administration of the district pertaining to the welfare of the tribal people.

The number of Doloiships or *Elakas* in Jaintia Hills in the earlier period was not constant due to some reasons. Pakem is of the opinion that at the beginning there were originally only three *Elakas*. Subsequently, the number increased to seven with the creation of another four *Elakas*. It was during this period of time when Jaintia Hills was administred by these seven *Dolois* that the Jaintias from the hills invaded the plains of Sylhet and conquered it. With the conquest of the southern plains, the territories of the *Dolois* obviously expanded. On account of this expansion and additional territories, the administrative duties and responsibilities of the *Dolois* also increased tremendously. Perhaps after having realised the difficulties to meet the various requirements of the ever increasing administration, both in the hills and plains, that an urgent need was felt necessary to create more *Elakas* to be administred by the *Dolois* themselves. In this way another five *Elakas* were created making it altogether twelve in number, each under the administration and supervision of a *Doloi*. Moreover, these twelve *Elakas* seemed to remain constant for a long period of time or until the British came and annexed the area. Perhaps on the basis of this number of *Elakas* that Jaintia Hills was called by its people as 'the Land of the Twelve *Dolois*' and came also to be known as such by its neighbours.[8] After the annexation of Jaintia Hills by the British in 1835, the number of *Elakas* further increased by them by breaking the existing *Elakas* into smaller ones. This process of division of the *Elakas* continued throughout the British rule over the area, that at a certain period of time there were as many as 25 such units in the whole of Jaintia Hills.

Bareh is of the opinion that at first there were five *Dolois*, next they increased to seven, and on the eve of the British annexation (of Jaintia Hills) they gave (*sic*) increase to twelve.[9] However, Bareh did not explain in clear terms as to why the number of Doloiships/*Elakas* had increased from what he said the original five to twelve. But he made an interesting observation in which he stated that it was only on the eve of the British annexation of Jaintia Hills that the number of Doloiships were found to be 12 in number. However, Pakem provides a different view altogether in this respect where he stated that in fact, the Jaintia *Elakas* increased from three to seven and from seven to 12 before the Jaintias formed a State (*Hima*). After the formation of the State, the *Elakas* further increased with further expansion or division until there were 25 *Elakas* during the British period.[10] The two views given above are quite different from each other and as far as the period is concerned, there is a wide gap between the two opinions. According to Pakem, the number of Doloiships reached to twelve in number before the Jaintias formed a State (*Hima*), or in other sense the period may be traced as far back as pre-State formation in Jaintia Hills. Unlike Pakem, Bareh opined that the period is not that of the distant past but it took place only on the eve of the British annexation of Jaintia Hills, that is, around the 1830s. Hadem, however, mentioned that the Jaintia King (which King?) divided his whole dominion into 12 administrative units called *Elakas*, under an administrator called *U Doloi*. He has also given the list of names of the 12 Doloiships which in his opinion regarded them to be the original ones. He was also of the opinion that on the basis of these twelve administrative units, the Jaintia Hills was termed as *Ka Ri Khad-ar Doloi* (the Land of the Twelve *Dolois*).[11]

As mentioned above, the number of Doloiships/*Elakas* increased from three to five, from five to seven and from seven to twelve. In the subsequent period more *Elakas* were created. A pertinent question arises as to why need was felt necessary to increase the number from time to time? And secondly, what are the reasons responsible for the creation of more *Elakas* in the area? Hadem has thrown some interesting insights as to the creation and division of some Doloiships in Jaintia Hills. This to some extent answers our queries as to how and in what manner, the uncrease in number of Doloiships from time to time took place. Hadem was of the opinion that one of the reasons responsible for such creation of new *Elakas* was due to internal fighting among the *Dolois*. The outcome of these unceasing troubles was a reward of independence to those areas where from their knights fought bravely for the defence of their parent *Elakas*. For example, Mynso area was granted an *Elaka* by the *Doloi* of

Shangpung; Raliang *Elaka* of course, by an accident, had to part with the area now called Shilliang-Myntang *Elaka* due to the blunder committed by the then Doloi of Raliang. The *Doloi* of this *Elaka*, for enjoyment's sake, carelessly put the 'Turban' (*Doloi's* crown) on the head of his son and the Council Elders (who were then present at that particular moment) immediately demanded that his son be declared a *Doloi* since he was allowed to put on the '*Doloi's* turban'. The *Doloi* had no other alternative than to yield to their demand in accordance with the traditional custom and part with the area of Shilliang-Myntang *Elaka*. Some of the present *Elakas* were split out of their parent *Elakas'* area by the British for their administrative conveniences and according to their policy of 'Divide and Rule'.[12]

It is also to be mentioned that some new *Elakas* were created with the permission of some of the Jaintia Kings out of love and affection for the people of a particular area because of their good deeds and the help they rendered to a particular king or his family members when they were facing a difficult situation or crisis in the hands of their enemies. The people of the village or area on hearing the news that their king or his family members had fallen victim to their enemies, immediately came to their rescue. One such outstanding example could be seen in the case of the creation of the Satpator *Elaka*. It was a practice that each *Elaka* from the hills has to pay an annual tribute of one he-goat to the King at Jaintiapur, the capital of the kingdom. In one such occasion, the people of Satpator brought their tribute of a he-goat, excellently decorated the animal and covered its horns with decorative pieces of silver. This excellent artistic style of performance by the people of the area drew the immediate attention of the King and all the more he appreciated this kind gesture. In appreciation of this kind gesture and good deed, the King honoured and rewarded the people by way of granting them permission to have their own separate *Elaka*. Thus a new *Elaka* was created with the actual name of "Sap-pitor", which literally means "silver clothe", originating from the silver covering on the horns of the he-goat. The *Elaka* was later on wrongly called as "Satpator" which name remains till today. Another outstanding example is the creation of a new *Elaka* for the area now under the Nongtalang *Elaka*. It was mentioned that once the sister of Rajah Borkusain II (1731–1770), Kong Rimai or

Korimai (Koari) was kidnapped and detained by the *Syiem* of Khyrim. The people of Nongbareh village, whose village falls within the jurisdiction of the Jaintia kingdom and which is also situated on the border of the area under the Khyrim Syiemship, came to help and managed to rescue the King's sister. They took her to their village. The royal lady after her rescue had to climb a difficult steep to reach Nongbareh village. When she finally reached the village, she wanted to have a glass of water to quench her thirst. It so happened that the family from whom she received a glass of pure honey belonged to the Lamin clan. The lady in the house, Ka Rontia Lamin, knowing that Kong Rimai or Korimai belonged to the royal family and she is also the King's sister, wanted to offer her the best she could provide to relieve the thirsty royal lady. So instead of offering a glass of water, she rather offered Kong Rimai a glass of pure honey. The royal lady was so glad to receive the honey and drank it all with full content. Because of this kind deed after her rescue, Kong Rimai then and there proclaimed to all that a new *Elaka* covering the area now under the jurisdiction of the present Nongtalang Doloiship be created. Moreover, she also granted the sole right that only the members from the clan of Ka Rontia Lamin will ever hold the office of the *Doloi* of Nongtalang. This is the reason how the new *Elaka* of Nongtalang came into existence. Since then the rights and privileges of holding the office of *Doloi* of Nongtalang *Elaka* continue to be enjoyed by the Lamin clan even today. All these incidents mentioned above throw light on how new *Elakas* or Doloiships were created and why the number of such *Elakas* in Jaintia Hills increased from time to time even before the coming of the British. Still, some new *Elakas* were created because of non-fulfilment of and/or inability to fulfil certain religious obligations. A clear example on this basis is that of Nongkhlieh *Elaka* when it was carved out of the Sutnga *Elaka*.[13]

On closer persual of the different sources relating to Jaintia history in general and Doloiships in particular, we get the impression that these sources can safely be divided into two broad categories — namely, those that informed us of the existence of only 12 *Elakas* or Doloiships and the other which clearly mentioned that there were more than 12 *Elakas* throughout Jaintia Hills. One of the sources which mentioned that Jaintia Hills consisted of only 12 divisions or units or Doloiships, was that of Syed Murtaza Ali as it appeared in his book *The History of Jaintia*. The names of the twelve divisions or Doloiships in the hilly portion of Jaintia Hills as provided in the book[14] are, namely — (Correct spelling of names is shown in brackets).

1. Suhtnga (Sutnga)
2. Nartiang
3. Jawai (Jowai)
4. Nongjhini (Nongjngi)
5. Shangpung
6. Raliang
7. Mynso
8. Natelang (Nongtalang)
9. Rambhai (Rymbai)
10. Lakhdong (Lakadong)
11. Nongbare (Nongbareh)
12. Non-pu (Narpuh)

It is interesting to note that while giving the list of names of 'the twelve divisions', Ali was very particular to make a mention that these divisions were only those of 'the hilly portion of Jaintia Hills'. This is because of the reason that the same author had the knowledge of the existence of other Doloiships in the plains or Jaintia Hills. There were three such Doloiships that existed in the plains during the reign of Ram Singh I (1701–1708). These were Mulagool, Jaflong and Charikhata.[15] If we consider this account given by Ali, we may therefore come to the conclusion that there were altogether 15 Doloiships in the hills and plains of the Jaintia kingdom during the time when it was ruled by Ram Singh I. Curiously, Ali was silent about the pattern of administration that prevailed in those Doloiships in the plains. One wonders whether the same type or pattern of administration that prevailed among the Doloiships in the hills was applied to them or it might be totally different. This needs further probing. J.B. Shadwell was also of the opinion that Jaintia Hills was divided into twelve 'separate communities', and under an officer called a *Doloi*.[16] He did not, however, explain as to why he preferred to use the term 'separate communities' than any other. The list of names of the twelve Doloiships was also not mentioned in his writing.

Whether Jaintia Hills was administered by the 12 *Dolois* before it formed a State (*Hima*) or the same took place only after one of the Kings himself divided his territory into 12 units or Doloiships, or it took place on the eve of its being taken over by the British, the fact remains that the number of *Elakas* fluctuated throughout the history of the area concerned. A.J.M. Mills mentioned that there were altogether 23 *Dolois* and Sirdars in the Jaintia Hills.[17] Like Shadwell, he also did not provide the list of names of these Doloiships and Sirdarships. Another British official, W.J. Allen, stated that Jaintia Hills was divided into 19 separate *Elakas*, fifteen of which were under the *Dolois* and the remaining four were under the charge of 13 Headmen called *Sirdars*.[18] Allen has also provided the list of names of these 15 Doloiships and four Sirdarships though he did not specifically mention against the names which one is Doloiship or Sirdarship. However, this can be easily differentiated by those who are aware of the status and position of these administrative units.

In 1860, twenty five years after the British annexation of Jaintia Hills, Capt. E.A. Rowlatt, then Principal Assistant Commissioner-in-charge of Khasi and Jaintia Hills, while submitting his memorandum of Demands, Collection and Balance of House Tax in Jaintia Hills to Colonel Jenkins, had shown the total number of *Elakas* as many as 21 where the demand for collection of the tax was made.[19] W.F. Trotter had mentioned that the Jaintia Hills territory was divided into 24 separate *Elakas* or circles, 19 of which were presided over by the *Dolois* and the remaining five were under the charge of Headmen called *Sirdars*.[20]

Of all the British officials and administrators who had given their reports on the administration of Jaintia Hills, W.W. Hunter has provided the most exhaustive list of names of Doloiships and Sirdarships in Jaintia Hills. His list consisted of 25 units of what he called 'fiscal divisions'.[21] Trotter had mentioned 24 such units, but Hunter added another one which was a Sirdarship in his list. Thus Hunter's list proved to be the most detailed one.

In 1884, Mr. Heath, the Sub-Divisional Officer of Jaintia Hills, while submitting his report on the land tenure in Jaintia Hills, mentioned the existence of 19 Doloiships and four Sirdarships.[22] P.R.T. Gurdon too, in 1907, mentioned the existence of 20 Doloiships and three Sirdarships.[23] The Census Report of 1911 gave the list of 20 Doloiships in the whole of Jaintia Hills.[24] C.U. Aitchison, in 1929, reported that Jaintia Hills after its annexation in 1835 was divided into 23 petty districts, 20 of which were in charge of elected Headmen, called *Dolois*; while the remaining three (reduced to two in 1910 by the amalgamation of two *Elakas*) were under hereditary *Sardars*.[25] Thus in this process, we find that the number of *Elakas* did not remain constant throughout the long past history of Jaintia Hills. A careful analysis of the records of the number of these *Elakas* or Doloiships as reported from time to time shows that the number of these *Elakas* fluctuated. But it also appears that at a particular period of time, the whole of Jaintia Hills had only 12 *Elakas*. This fact remains generally accepted and on this basis Jaintia Hills is sometimes referred to as *Ka Ri Khad-ar Doloi* (The Land of the Twelve *Dolois*). However, after the British had taken over the administration and their possession of the whole of Jaintia Hills, they further split and created more number of *Elakas* that at a certain point of time, there were as many as 25 such administrative units in Jaintia Hills including that of Sirdarships created by the British.

Coming to the period after Independence, the information contained in the United Khasi-Jaintia Hills Autonomous District Act, 1953, mentioned that there were 18 Doloiships and one Sirdarship in the whole of Jaintia Hills. The same number of Doloiships and Sirdarships was shown by the same District Council Act of 1959. Curiously, one Patorship, that of Sumer, was missing in both the lists. But in the present list available with the Jaintia Hills Autonomous District Council, there are 18 Doloiships, one Sirdarship and one Patorship.

REFERENCES

1. Pakem, B. 'State Formation in Pre-Colonial Jaintia', *The North-Eastern Hill University Journal of Social Sciences and Humanities*, (hereafter NEHU Journal), NEHU Publications, Vol. II, No. 3, July–September 1984, Shillong, p. 52.
2. *Ibid.*
3. Pakem, B. 'The Changing Power Structure of the Political Institutions of Jaintia Chieftainship', *The Journal of North-East India Council for Social Science Research* (hereafter *NEICSSR Journal*), Vol. I, No. I, April 1977, Shillong, p. 1.
4. Pakem, B. *op. cit., NEHU Journal*, p. 52.
5. *Ibid.*
6. *Ibid.*, p. 53; see also B. Pakem; *NEICSSR Journal, op cit.*, p. 1.

7. Pakem, B. *op cit., NEHU Journal*, p. 50.
8. Discussion with Dr. B. Pakem.
9. Bareh, Hamlet. *The History and Culture of the Khasi People*, Shillong 1967, p. 63.
10. Pakem, B. 'A Theoretical Approach to the Study of State and Polity Formation in Meghalaya during the Pre-colonial period with special reference to Jaintia State and Biate Chieftaincy', Seminar paper on 'Pre-History of Meghalaya and Social Formation in Khasi-Jaintia Hills', Education Department, Government of Meghalaya, 23–24 April 1985 (Mimeograph).
11. Hadem, Humphrey. 'Suggestions and Objections to the proposed Delimitation of the 7 Legislative Assembly Constituencies for Jaintia Hills', 3rd. December 1974 (Mimeograph).
12. *Ibid.*
13. Pakem, B. *op cit.* (Note 10).
14. Ali, Syed Murtaza. *The History of Jaintia*, Dacca 1954, p. 1.
15. *Ibid.*, p. 29.
16. Shadwell, J.B. *Note on the Inhabitants of the Khasi and Jaintia Hills*, 1871, Assam Secretariat Printing Office, Shillong, p. 8.
17. Mills, A.J.M. *Report on the Khasi and Jaintia Hills*, 1853, Assam Secretariat Printing Office (Reprint), Shillong 1901, p. 7.
18. Allen, W.J. *Report on the Administration of the Cossyah and Jynteah Hill Territory*, 1858, Government Press (Reprint), Shillong 1975, p. 65.
19. Home Department Public Consultation A, 13 October 1860, No. 60, Rowlatt to Jenkins, 11 May 1860.
20. Trotter, W.F. *Report on the Administration of Jowai for the year ending 31st March* 1878, Calcutta 1878, p. 15.
21. Hunter, W.W. *A Statistical Account of Assam*, Vol. II, B.R. Publishing Corporation (Reprint), Delhi 1975, p.
22. Cantlie, Sir Keith. *Notes on Khasi Law* (Ed. and Reprinted) by A.S. Khongphai, Shillong 1974, p. 104.
23. Gordon, P.R.T. *The Khasis*, Cosmo Publications (Reprint), New Delhi 1981, p. 75.
24. Sarma-Roy, B.K. *Ka Histori Jong Ka Ri Khasi*, Shillong 1914.
25. Aitchison, C.U. *Collection of Treaties, Engagements and Sanads Relating to India and Neighbouring Countries*, Vol. XII, Mittal Publications (Reprint), Delhi 1983, p. 83.

CHAPTER II

Methods of Election of a *Doloi*

A *Doloi* is usually elected from among the adult male members of the original or founding clan or clans (*Kurs*) of the *Elaka* or Province. Further, even from among the original clan or clans, the candidate or candidates for the elective post of a *Doloi* were recruited mostly on ascriptive criteria rather than on grounds of achievements.[1] However, as far as 'election' is concerned, it cannot be attributed to be based on ascriptive criteria, but on achievement basis. It is true of course, that candidates to the office of *Doloi* must be the members of the original clan or clans.

In the case of Jaintia traditional polity and social stratification, we find that the original or founding clans have a special place and role to play. These clans are regarded as such because it was they who were the first or earliest settlers in a village or *Elaka*. Since it was these colonising clans who possibly first occupied and cleared the forests and lands for settlement, they also became the proprietor of the land. They were also entitled with permanent ownership of that land. The principle of treating the founder-members as owners of landed property and secondly the principle of right of landownership for the rulers who constituted political power and for the people who symbolised political authority, came into existence.[2] The original clans also became the legitimate ruling clans within the area under their jurisdiction and extended their protection to new or late-comers who joined and settled within their fold. Such clans are regarded as *Ki Khian Kur*, literally small clans or outsiders. Moreover, exclusive rights and privileges were granted only to the members of the original clans for setting up of candidates for the office of *Doloi*. The *Khian Kurs* are deprived of such right and privileges. Against this background, we find that only the original clans or *Kmai Kur* (big clan) within their respective *Raids* could produce leaders and whose members could also aspire for any political office of significance in the *Raid*.[3] The *Khian Kur* would not have any say in the running of the political affairs of the *Raid*, except the right to vote in the election of the *Doloi* or *Pator*. The original clans or *Kmai Kur* are usually referred to by the total number of clans as *Ki Soo Kpoh* (four clans) of Jowai and were later on joined by some more clans, or *Ki Ynniaw Kur* (seven clans) of Sumer, or *Ki La Poh* (three clans)[4] from the villages of Lamin, Nongtalang and Nongbareh and who are the descendants of *Ka law Shibia* or *Ka law Shibidi*. These clans only have the right to occupy the office of the *Doloi* of Nongtalang *Elaka*.

An *Elaka* was and is still incharge of a political head with the designation of *U Doloi* or a Provincial Governor assisted in some *Elakas* by *U Pator* or a Lieutenant Governor. In the case of nomination or setting up of candidates to either office of *Doloi* or *Pator*, only the traditional original clans have the sole right and privilege to do so. For example, in the Jowai *Elaka*, the *Doloi* was nominated by the members of the *Soo Kpoh* and later on by the other clans as well and elected by all the adult male members of the *Elaka*. In Sumer, the *Pator* was nominated by the *Ynniaw Kur* and elected by all the adult male members of the Sumer Patorship of the Raliang *Elaka*.[5] In the Nongtalang *Elaka*, the *Doloi* is nominated by the members of the *La Poh* of Lamin, Nongtalang and Nongbareh villages and accordingly elected by all the adult male members of the *Elaka*. Against this background, it may be noted that no one could be nominated and appointed as a *Doloi* or *Pator* unless he belongs to one of the original clans of the *Elaka*. The members of the other clans and/or the general population, who are considered as outsiders or *Khian Kur* in the *Elaka* could not aspire to an elective post and would not have any say in the actual running of the political affairs of the *Elaka*, accept the right to vote in such an election.

However, there has been attempts made by the members of the non-original clans in the past and in recent times to put forward their claims over the right to office of a *Doloi*. Occasionally and in a very few cases especially during the British period, even members of such clans were elected to the office of a *Doloi*. But that was only a temporary arrangement. For instance, way back in the year 1909, it was reported that U Khein, an ex-*Doloi* or Shangpung *Elaka* was prohibited by the Deputy Commissioner, Khasi and Jaintia Hills, from standing for election. He tried to cause trouble by advocating the claims of his clan, that is, the Papang clan, to eligibility to the office of *Doloi* in the *Elaka*. This clan, as according to the customary practices, was clearly ineligible, and U Khein's election on a previous occasion was due to a misunderstanding. In consequence, however, of U Khein's representations, the Deputy Commissioner was himself present at the elections at Shangpung. There were three candidates for the Doloiship, and under the arrangements of Mr. S.E. Rita, the Subdivisional Officer of Jowai, the election went off quite peacefully. It was further reported that there did not seem to be any desire locally either for U Khein or any other Papang *Doloi*.[6] Such a claim which does not have the sanction of the traditional custom and usages of the land, proved only to be a failure. In another recent instance, in the election of an acting *Doloi* in the Sutnga Doloiship, the elected person does not belong to the *Doloi* clan whereas the defeated candidate is one. But such an incumbent will be only for a temporary period, pending the disposal of the charges against the *Doloi*, or in case he is dismissed, pending the regular election.[7]

A much recent phenomenon has also developed among the Jaintia people, though in a very mild form, that is, the demand made by some non-original clans in few *Elakas* for granting equal 'opportunity' in the case of setting up of candidates to the offices of *Doloi* and *Pator*. In those *Elakas* where such a demand has taken place, the non-original clans tried to bring in the modern concept of democratisation of elections and the right to setting up of candidates be granted to all the clans within the *Elaka*, irrespective whether they belong to the original or non-original clans. Thus, the non-original clans are against the idea, practice and 'opportunity' being concentrated and limited only to those members of particular original clans of the *Elaka*. This, in a sense is a threat to the traditional customary practice and the traditional political system which has emerged since time immemorial within the society itself. Such a development could be cited in a very recent instance which took place in 1987 in the Nongtalang *Elaka*. In this particular *Elaka*, after the death of the former *Doloi*, the members of one of the non-original clans, the Myrchiang clan from Nongtalang village, put a claim of right to the office of *Doloi* in the *Elaka*. The members of this clan submitted a petition to the authorities of the Jaintia Hills Autonomous District Council stating among other things that the members of their clan had been appointed *Doloi* once upon a time by the Jaintia *Syiem*. But nowhere the record shows that such an incident took place. However, the matter is still lying pending for decision by the District Council authorities. This speaks of the existing phenomenon today where such claim of right has emerged from among the non-original clans. However, the Jaintia society as a whole has not as yet accepted such kind of demand to bring in a drastic change in their traditional customary practices. In the final analysis, even when such occasional deviation has taken place in the society, but it proved to be a total failure.

Once a *Doloi* is elected, he normally holds the office for the rest of his life. Traditionally and till the advent of the British, the tenure of office was for a life time. However, a *Doloi* may be punished, expelled or asked to resign, should he arouse sufficient hostility to the people of the *Elaka*. If a *Doloi* shows some kind of misbehaviour towards the people by inflicting unduly harsh punishments or irrationally suppressed them which may be against the norms of the society, and the people feel collectively that such inflictions are not according to the law, customs and usages of the land, they have the right and authority to strip the *Doloi* of his office. The *Dolois* could not therefore misbehave towards their people. The people may appeal to their *Langdohs* if the *Dolois* had oppressed them in any way contrary to the age-old norms of the society they live in. And if the *Dolois* were found guilty, they might be removed accordingly.[8] A *Doloi* who tried petty tyranny would soon find himself a chief without any followers. For example, in the case of the *Doloi* of Jowai *Elaka*, the decision to punish him for his misdeeds may be taken even by the people of the four Langdohships only and not necessarily by the whole *Elaka* population.[9] Even during the period when Jaintia Hills was under the British rule, many *Dolois* were dismissed from their office on the basis of the complaints filed against such erring *Dolois* by the people of their respective *Elakas*. For example, in the year 1907-1908, the Deputy Commissioner, Khasi and Jaintia Hills, dismissed U Shan, *Doloi* of Shangpung, as unsuited to continue in his office on the basis of the unfavourable report and several complaints filed against him by his people.[10] In another case, U Manik, *Doloi* of Darang *Elaka*, had to resign from office in 1892, as he did not find favour with his people.[11]

Ceremonies of Investiture

With a view to legitimise the functions of the office, the *Dolois* in Jaintia Hills were offered ceremonies and other investitures after their election. Some of these rites pertaining to the investitures of the doloiship are still followed and performed in certain *Elakas*. In such investitures and religious performances in connection with the occasion, water is sprinkled, head-gear girded, prayers are offered, presents are exchanged and oath of allegiance are taken to. High priests or authorised spokesmen often perform the task of annointing the elected ruler-administrator of the people. Bareh recorded the investiture ceremony thus:

> "During his (*Doloi*) investiture, he is mounted over a sacred stone slab in the market of his headquarters where the head of the *Pator* clan approaches him, and girds a head-dress round his head citing solemn addresses. An exchange of addresses follow. Liqour and betels are distributed, accompanied by sprinkling of sacred water. In Jowai, the investiture ceremony is closed by the handing over of a rod to the new *Doloi* by the *Lyngdoh* (*Langdoh*). In Sutnga it is closed by decorating the *Doloi's* ears with the precious metal by representatives of the five *Khers* (clans) — Pala, Suja, Lamare, Sutnga and Basan. In Shangpung the 12 *Khers* anoint him decorating his neck with a water pearl and presenting him a silver cup. . . The new *Doloi* in the past used to receive a *tola* of gold from the *Syiem* as an act of confirmation being appointed to office by his people on the merit of election."[12]

REFERENCES

1. Pakem, B. 'The Changing Power Structure of the Political Institutions of Jaintia Chieftainship', *NEICSSR Journal, op. cit.*, p. 2.
2. Pakem, B. A Theoretical Approach to the Study of State and Polity Formation in Meghalaya during the Pre-Colonial Period with special reference to Jaintia State and Biate Chieftaincy', 1985 (Mimeograph).
3. Pakem, B. 'State Formation in Pre-Colonial Jaintia', *NEHU Journal, op. cit.*, p. 52.
4. *Ibid*.
5. *Ibid*.

6. *General Administration Report of the Khasi and Jaintia Hills District for the year ending 31st. March 1909; No. 867, Shillong, 12 May 1909;* L.O. Clarke to the Commissioner Surma Valley and Hill Districts, p. 6.
7. Pakem, B. 'Meghalaya: Some Aspects of Political Development' in *North East India: A Sociological Study*, S.M. Dubey (Ed.), Concept Publishing Company, Delhi 1978, p. 239.
8. Pakem, B. *op. cit.* (Note 1).
9. Laloo, S.S. *Ka Behdienkhlam* (no date), p. 256.
10. *Annual Report on the Administration of Khasi and Jaintia Hills for the year 1907-08*; No. 484, Shillong, 3 April 1908, Jackson to the Commissioner Surma Valley and Hill Districts.
11. *Political Report of the Khasi and Jaintia Hills District for 1890–93*; Assam Secretariat, Forgn. A. Progs., July 1893, Nos. 22–23; Gray to the Secretary to the Chief Commissioner of Assam, No. 902, Shillong, 11 April 1893.
12. Bareh, Hamlet. *The History and Culture of the Khasi People*, Shillong 1967, p. 257.

CHAPTER III

Powers and Functions

Pre-British Period

The *Dolois* in Jaintia Hills are not autocratic rulers and have no dictatorial power over the people of their respective *Raids* or *Elakas*. Their provinces are really republics though very tiny indeed. Like the *Syiem* or Raja, the *Dolois* also have to rule according to the popular opinion of their respective *Elakas*. This is clearly noticed from the fact that all actions initiated or taken by a *Doloi* would have to be approved by all the citizens of the *Elaka*, through the general *durbar* (*Durbar Raid* or *Elaka*).[1] Thus in the pre-British period, power belonged not only to the *Dolois*, but also shared by their people. The people appointed their rulers to supervise their activities.[2] The people therefore elected their chiefs in order to supervise the administration and not to suppress or oppress them. For sometime even after the British Political Agent was appointed to look after and conduct the affairs of administration of Jaintia Hills, he granted permission to the people of the area to elect, retain and remove their *Dolois* according to their own traditional customary practices.

With the annexation of the Jaintia parganas in the plains of Sylhet (now in Bangladesh) in the south and Nowgong plains in the north to the Jaintia kingdom through conquest, the Jaintia *Syiems* thus ruled over the people both in the hills and the plains. But the *Syiem's* personal rule and authority prevailed only over the conquered territories of the plain areas. In the hills section of the Jaintia kingdom, the administration was left entirely in the hands and supervision of the *Dolois*; the *Syiem* in this case acted only as a titular head. The only symbol of allegiance and the semblance of power which the *Syiem* had enjoyed over the *Dolois* from the hills was an annual tribute of one he-goat from each *Elaka* under their administration. But this was more ceremonial or religious than political, though technically, a tribute system is symbolic of a basic power structure. The *Syiem* was no more than a symbol of unity of the people; and if his activities threatened that unity, the latter would strongly oppose him.[3] The he-goats received by the *Syiem* from the *Dolois* were used for religious sacrifices at Rajbari in Jaintiapur, the capital of the kingdom.

With regard to internal organisation and in order to maintain proper and smooth administration, the hills portion of the Jaintia kingdom was split into several administrative units or *Elakas*. Each of these *Elakas* was and is still looked after by the *Doloi*.

When the office of the *Syiem* was in existence, the Jaintia *Syiems* considered the *Dolois* as important administrators or ministers of the hill areas of the kingdom since it were the latter who actually run and supervised the entire administration in the hills. The *Dolois* being powerful heads of the hills administrative units, served the *Syiems* in those days in the capacity of military commanders, as well as ministers and even as ambassadors to foreign courts, especially that of the Ahom court. Whenever engaged in exercising their functions as ministers, they stayed at Jaintiapur,[4] the seat of the capital. Moreover, the *Dolois* used to spend half of the year at Jaintiapur to assist the *Syiem* in his administration. During their absence, the *Dolois* entrusted to *Pators* or Deputy-Governors, the management and administration of their respective *Elakas*. The *Syiem* also used to convene the *Dolois* to his court where State Councils were held for settling problems arising out of inter-*Elaka* relations.[5] Acting as the revenue officers of the *Syiem*, the *Dolois* were entrusted the task of collecting revenue as well as supervised the collections of ceremonial presents and acknowledgement gifts of subject residents to the *Syiem*.[6]

The *Dolois* had certain executive, political, judicial and religious functions to perform within their respective jurisdiction. In the past, they also performed military functions. Besides extending their hands in assisting the *Syiem* in his administration, the *Dolois* on their part executed and exercised important decisions in matters relating to the administration and welfare of the people in their respective *Elakas*. In running the administration of his *Elaka*, the *Doloi* was and is still assisted and guided by the *Durbar Elaka* or *Durbar Raid* and an executive council consisting of leading persons like the *Pator*, the *Wasan*, the *Dan* (collector), the *Duhalia* (musician), the *Sangot* (village crier), and others.[7] The *Doloi* could either function directly or through his deputy, the *Pator*, with the assistance of *Ki Tymmen Ki San* (Elders) or simply *Ki Wasan*. *Ki Wasan* were the elders, one each from every clan in the *Raid*, acting as representatives of their respective clans.[8] The *Doloi* although being the chief of the *Elaka* cannot act or decide things all by himself. Any decision concerning the *Elaka* has to be approved by the *Durbar Elaka*.

The *Dolois* wielded much power over their respective *Elakas*. In the hills section of the Jaintia kingdom, as the administration was left entirely in the hands and supervision of the *Dolois*, they could allow the *Syiem* to handle only matters of common interests like defence, communications and foreign affairs and that too in a very limited way. For example, the *Doloi* could take over foreign affairs from the *Syiem* in his absence or if his policy was at variance with that of the *Dolois*. There was a case when the Ahoms had captured Raja Ram Singh I (1694–1708) upon which the hill people rose against the Ahoms even during the absence of their *Syiem*.[9] Another example that can be cited here was what happened when Raja Borkussain II or Bar Gossain II (1731–1770), his sister Kong Rimai (Gauri or Kauri), Mon Myngngor and Sekhising were arrested and detained at Nongkrem by the Raja of Khyrim.[10] The Jaintia people rose against the *Syiem* of Khyrim to set free their own *Syiem*.

The *Dolois* and their people could even take a decision to do away with a *Syiem* if he so incurred displeasure or acted in a ruthless manner against them. For instance, one of such incidents took place during the reign of Raja Bejoy Narayan (1782–1788). It was mentioned that, during the reign of this king, Urpang, the *Doloi* of Nartiang had a handsome looking son, Laxmi by name. The king's sister, Barkuari, took a fancy to him and got him appointed as *Munsif*, who in those days was entrusted with the duty of counting fuel supplied free to the king by his people. Laxmi was a clever person and soon obtained great ascendancy at the court. The king would consult him in important matters and listened to his advice. This created enormous jealousy and enmity amongst the courtiers who hatched a conspiracy against Laxmi. In those days, *Rajbadua* (the Royal informer) was very much trusted by the kings. The courtiers won *Rajbadua* over and induced him to tell the king that Laxmi was carrying an intrigue with the king's sister. The king became enraged (when he was told) and immediately ordered the apprehension of Laxmi. Laxmi however managed to remain in hiding. The king ordered all the *Laskars* to keep watch over Nijpat so that Laxmi could not escape.

However, inspite of the tight security, one day at midnight when the people of Jaintiapur had been encircled by watchmen appointed by the king to prevent escape of Laxmi, the king's sister (Barkuari) secured the escape of Laxmi by inducing Khadhan Laskar of Chatul to allow passage to Laxmi. She personally requested Khadhan to grant a passage of exit to Laxmi. Khadhan was unwilling to refuse the request from a princess of royal blood. Next morning, the king discovered that Laxmi had slipped through the area under Khadhan's charge and sent for him. Khadhan admitted his guilt and was executed under royal command.

When Laxmi's mother learnt of the services rendered by Khadhan, she started for Jaintiapur with seven loads of silver coins, as presents for Khadhan. On the way she came to learn of the death of Khadhan and threw all the money (silver coins) into a pit in annoyance. The chieftains of Jaintia Hills assembled and took serious objection to the king's attempt to capture Laxmi. The hill people even decided to boycott the Jaintia people (in the plains) and stopped all trading relations. This state of affairs continued for three years. Thereafter, the chieftains of the hills and plains conspired to do away with the king and install Laxmi Singh in his place. The king who was very fond of boat race, was invited to a boat race in kendri *bil* and was treacherously done to death. Thereafter Laxmi Singh was installed on the throne of Jaintia.[11]

In another incident which shows that the *Dolois* could openly rebel against their *Syiem* if the latter happened to misbehave towards the former, took place between Raja Rajendra Singh (1832–1835) and the *Dolois* of Jowai and Nartiang. However, Lt. Inglis of the East India Company saved the situation by bringing the two parties together and settled the matter peacefully.[12] In extreme cases, the *Dolois* and their people could even resort to regicide. The last example of regicide in *Ri Jaintia* was that of Raja Ban Singh (1660–1669) who was put to death by his hill people on the recommendation of the priest before whom the complaints against Raja Ban Singh's tyrannical acts were made.[13] The priest seemed therefore, to have enjoyed the ultimate power over the rulers in *Ri Jaintia*.[14]

The *Dolois* also performed judicial functions. A *Doloi* of an *Elaka* acted as a judge and the members of the *Elaka* court as a jury while trying or deciding cases involving the people of the *Elaka* concerned. In the past, a *Doloi* tried all sorts of cases, both of simple and serious nature like theft, robbery, murder, rape, dacoity, cattle-stealing, arson, house-breaking, etc. He was to put into trial all those who committed heinous crimes within the jurisdiction of his *Elaka*. However, after the British annexation of Jaintia Hills in 1835, most of the judicial powers and functions of the *Dolois* were either curtailed to a great extent or taken away. Cases of serious nature, especially those involving heinous crimes, could no longer be tried by them. Such cases were to be tried by the British Political Agent or the Assistant Commissioner or the Deputy Commissioner as the case may be. The British authorities granted the *Dolois* permission to try those cases upto the amount of Rs. 50 only. 'The *Dolois* had, therefore, magisterial and police powers and with the decision of the full doloiship *durbar*, they settled cases and inflicted fines and penalties on criminals.'[15]

Traditionally, by virtue of his descent, a *Doloi* is the link between his people and the supernatural spirits governing their welfare. As the leader of the people and the head of certain privilege or founding clans, he also plays the religious role in an ancestral cult. During the ceremonies and festivals which are common in Jaintia Hills, a *Doloi* plays an important religious role whenever necessary. However, in religious matters, not all the *Dolois* perform this function. In some *Elakas*, the *Dolois* do perform the dual functions, both religious and secular; whereas in other *Elakas*, the *Doloi* does not perform any such religious function at all. In such *Elakas*, there are other officials who are entrusted with such religious functions. The dual functions of a *Doloi*, therefore differ from one *Elaka* to another. For example, in the Nongtalang Elaka, the *Doloi* does not perform any religious function. Some *Dolois* of this *Elaka* were also Christians.

In those *Elakas* where the *Doloi* performs such religious functions while observing certain festivals, he acts as the head of the *Langdohs* (priests). For instance, for sometime in the Jowai *Elaka*, the *Doloi's* presence while performing such religious functions was necessary. During the *Behdienkhlam* festival of the Jaintias, he used to attend to all the religious ceremonies. Moreover, in all such religious ceremonies the *Doloi* was helped and assisted by the *Wasans* of the *Elaka*. But during the time when Ram Lato was the *Doloi* of Jowai, he was converted into Christianity. Therefore the people of the Jowai *Elaka* has to appoint a *Doloi Niam* or a *Doloi* meant only for religious purposes. Such a *Doloi* has nothing to do with the secular or administrative affairs of the *Elaka*. In the past, 'in Sutnga Doloiship, five important sacrifices are held in a year, but the most important observance is the market *poojah* (*Pam Iaw*) which is a sacrifice of goats to the deities. The *Doloi* of Sutnga and a local priest conducted these ceremonies. Another popular sacrifice is the *Pyrda*, where prayers are offered to invoke the help of a water-goddess. Prior to this observance, preliminary rites called *Nguh-Blei* (or *Nguh-Blai* in Jaintia) are performed. In this ceremony, the *Doloi* is mounted over a stone and after some days are passed, the celebration of *Pyrda* is observed. The important ceremony in the Shangpung Doloiship is connected with the Mawshai goddess (market deity) to whom 30 sacrifices are offered.'[16]

A *Doloi* is paid no salary, but is provided with a large section of the land known as *Rek* for his maintenance during the term of service. But in the southern part of the Jaintia Hills District, that is in the War area, there are no such provisions of *Rek* lands. In the absence of such lands, the *Dolois* in the War area *Elakas* do not enjoy any such privilege like their counterparts in the other *Elakas*, especially those in the northern part of the District. In some *Elakas*, the *Dolois* still share the market imposts with their officials. A portion of these imposts is however utilised for meeting the expenses for observing market religious ceremonies. The collector of the market tolls is called *Dan*.[17]

Thus we find that with regards to their powers and functions, and 'in their own domains, the *Dolois* were more autocratic than even the Raja's rule over his people in the hills. To all intents and purposes, they were feudal despots. It was true that the institution of Doloiship had a semblance of democratic nature as a political system. But then this was confined only to the original clans. The general population could not aspire to the elective post of a *Doloi* . . . Operationally, however, as in the case of the Raja, the *Dolois* could not misbehave towards their people. Their people may appeal to their *Langdohs* if the *Dolois* had oppressed them in any way. And if the *Dolois* were found guilty, they might be removed accordingly.'[18]

So far as the other tiers of administration like the *Pator* in a Patorship, and *Waheh Chnong* in a village are concerned, these are under the control of the *Doloi* of an *Elaka*. Only matters of purely local concern had been left to be managed by them in their respective jurisdiction. But this does not mean that they could enjoy more powers without limit. In practice, and according to tradition, no category of rulers in Jaintia Hills, be he a *Syiem*, a *Doloi*, a *Pator* or a *Waheh Chnong* could become oppressive beyond a certain limit for fear of being removed from their office by the people. Nor could the people take the law into their own hands since they should have the recommendation of the priest for removing any of their rulers.[19]

REFERENCES

1. Pakem, B. 'The Socio-Political System of the Jaintia Tribe of Assam: An Analysis of Continuity and Change', in K. Suresh Singh (Ed.), *Tribal Situation in India*, IIAS, Simla 1972, p. 353.
2. *Census of India*, 1961, Vol. III, Part VI, No. 13, p. 29.
3. Pakem, B. *op. cit.*,
4. Bareh, Hamlet. *The History and Culture of the Khasi People*, Shillong 1967, pp. 267, 279.
5. *Ibid.*, p. 267.
6. *Ibid.*, 286.
7. Pakem, B. *NEICSSR Journal. op. cit.*, p. 2.
8. Pakem, B. *op cit.*
9. Pakem, B. *NEICSSR Journal, op. cit.*, p. 2.
10. Lyngdoh, U Homiwell. *Ki Syiem Khasi and Synteng*, Shillong 1964, pp. 70–74.
11. Ali, S.M. *The History of Jaintia*, Dacca 1954, pp. 48–49.
12. Pakem, B. *NEICSSR Journal, op. cit.*, p. 2.
13. Bareh, H. *op. cit.*, p. 73; see also Pakem, *Ibid*.
14. Pakem, B. *op. cit.*
15. Bareh, H. *op. cit.*, p. 279.
16. Bareh, H. *Khasi Democracy*, Shillong 1964, pp. 95–97.
17. Bareh, H. *op. cit.*, p. 279.
18. Pakem, B. *NEICSSR Journal, op. cit.*, p. 2.
19. *Ibid.*

CHAPTER IV

Effects of British Administration on the Powers and Functions of Dolois

In this chapter, the powers and functions of *Dolois* are being discussed keeping in view the effects of the British administration on the former's traditional powers and functions.

Before the coming of the British, the Jaintias had a three-tier system of government and administration. At the top of the hierarchy, there was the *Syiem* or *Raja* (*Syiem* to his people in the hills and *Raja* to his *ryots* in the plains); *Dolois* occupied the second place in the rung of the ladder of administration and the lowest hierarchy was occupied by the village Headman or *Waheh Chnong*. The British took over the administration of Jaintia Hills after its annexation in 1835, first under the East India Company and later on the area was placed under the British Crown. Certain new changes were brought by the British in the administrative system, which was hitherto supervised and administered by different heads of the indegeneous institutions of the people of the area under study. Immediately after the annexation, the office of the *Syiem* was abolished and therefore lapsed in 1835 itself. However, the offices of the *Doloi*, *Pator* and village Headman were retained by the British and initially allowed to continue as autonomous heads of their *Elakas* and villages respectively; but these too were stripped of many of their powers and functions in the subsequent years following the British decision to get themselves totally involved in the administrative affairs of Jaintia Hills.

In the hills section of the Jaintia kingdom, the administration of the country in the pre-British period was left entirely in the hands of the *Dolois* and other subordinate officials. As far as the hills section of the kingdom is concerned, the *Syiem* or *Raja* acted only as the nominal head of the State. The real power was possessed by the *Dolois*. They were at the head of the civil, criminal and police establishments of their respective *Elakas*. The village Headmen were under them and with such powers they were generally the real heads of the government and administration. This power relationship between the *Syiem* and the *Dolois* was also duly recognised by the British officials after they came forward to take over the administration. The only symbol of the *Dolois'* allegiance to the *Syiem* was an annual tribute of one he-goat from each *Elaka* under their administration.[1] It was also reported that *Raja* Indra Singh received a few seers of parched rice from most of the villages every year and a few bundles of firewood from the places where the wood is found. These articles were expended at the *pujas* at Rajbari in Jaintiapur. Moreover, every village in turn had to supply the *Raja* with coolies or porters and other servants for cultivating the Raj lands, and other purposes. He had some perquisites also from fees, fines, and *nussurs* presented to him on various occasions by the people of the hills.[2] It is possible that dues levied on hill produce imported to the plains formed a further source of income.[3] This symbol of allegiance was rather ceremonial than political, though technically, a tribute system is symbolic of a basic power system.[4] During the Colonial rule, the *Dolois* were asked to continue the payment of such annual tribute of he-goats to the British authorities at Cherrapunji instead of taking them as usual during the *Raja*'s time to Jaintiapur.

Changes Made on Tenure of Office

The age-old tenure of office of the *Doloi* came under a drastic change after the British decided to get themselves totally involved in the administration of the area. Of course, for quite sometime after the British took possession of the country, the British Political Agent appointed in the area permitted the people to elect, retain, and remove their *Dolois* according to their own traditional fashion. But subsequently, the Political Agent, in his own analysis of the situation, found it not suitable and convenient to allow this traditional practice of the people to continue any further. He therefore tried to find out some ways and means to put an end to the prevailing system of election conducted by the people.

How far the report given by the official concerned is true or false, cannot be ascertained, for according to one such report, 'there was a perpetual struggle between the influential inhabitants of many of the *Elakas* to procure the dismissal of the *Dolois* in office, and to replace him by some other candidates of an opposite faction. These frequent electioneering struggles kept the country in a constant turmoil, and produced much ill blood among the different classes of the people, without any corresponding advantage.'[5] In his own analysis of the situation which might have prevailed in Jaintia Hills during that time, the Political Agent proposed to stop it in order to maintain a healthy atmosphere of administration suited for the British to conduct their administrative business. Thus, subsequently, 'the Political Agent, in November 1850, passed an order that, for the future, persons elected and appointed *Dolois*, were to hold their offices for three years, provided they conducted their duties efficiently; at the end of every three years a new election was to take place, but the former *Doloi* might be re-elected as often as the people choose to elect him.'[6] Such orders passed by the British authorities surely created a big chasm between the traditional practice of the people and the British innovative plans.

Thus after Jaintia Hills became a British possession in 1835 and put under the latter's administration, the *Elakas* continued to be under the charge of the *Dolois*. However, the method of their election had changed. During this period of time, the *Dolois* were 'nominated' by the inhabitants of their respective *Elakas*, and were to be confirmed by the Prinicipal Assistant Commissioner, otherwise their election to the office will not be a valid one. The British authorities changed the traditional practice of 'election' to that of 'nomination' by the people in respect of appointing a new *Doloi* of an *Elaka*. Under the new circumstances and unlike the traditional practice; the *Dolois* were to hold office for a period of three years only, after the expiration of which another general election or rather nomination of *Dolois* takes place. The electorate were, however, allowed the freedom of choice, and 'their nominees were never rejected by the Cherra Authorities, unless they were in some manner notoriously disqualified for the office.'[7] W.J. Allen claimed that this action of effecting the change from life tenure to three years only in the case of appointment of the *Dolois* in Jaintia Hills was 'an improvement on the former practice and the *Dolois* felt secured because they will remain in office for three years only if they behave properly. Under the former regime they were liable to be turned adrift at any moment, and were obliged to be entirely subservient to those who had the power of ejecting them from office.'[8]

G.D. Showers, the Commissioner of Khasi and Jaintia Hills expressed his agreement to the above suggestion made by W.J. Allen. Moreover, as far as the native element of the government is concerned, he agreed to maintain it, but with slight changes. He recognised the *Dolois* as the head of the native element of the government. He was of the opinion that this office should continue to be held for three years according to the existing Rules in force, but the appointment, instead of being vacated at the end of that time, should only be reconsidered, except in the event of either the Superintendent-in-charge of the district or the village community being dissatisfied, when a new election should be ordered.[9]

B.W.D. Morton, the Deputy Commissioner-in-charge of Khasi and Jaintia Hills, did not agree on many of the suggestions put forward both by Allen and Showers. With regards to the method of election of *Dolois,* he was of the opinion that they should be selected by the people. As far as the tenure of office of the *Doloi* is concerned, he rejected both Allen and Showers opinions. He rather wanted to keep the *status quo* of the traditional practice by suggesting that, 'their (*Dolois*) appointment should be for life, or during good behaviour, and liable to cancelment by the Deputy Commissioner on regular investigation of alleged malpractice.'[10]

The changes made and proposed to be made in the tenure of office of the *Dolois* by the British authorities were not altogether free from objection and criticism by the holders of the office. For example, U Don, the *Doloi* of Jowai, fervently objected to the system of election for a period of three years only and asserted that the bulk of the population disliked it. This was of course outrightly rejected by W.J. Allen, the Member of the Board of Revenue.[11]

Imposition of Other Changes

Not satisfied only with the change in the tenure of office of the *Dolois*, the British authorities went further to the extent of not even allowing the *Dolois* 'to absent themselves from their districts for more than six months, without the permission of the Principal Assistant Commissioner.'[12] It may be noted here that, before the coming of the British, the *Dolois* were obliged to remain in attendance for about six months in a year, on the Jaintia *Raja* at Jaintiapur, and during this period of absence, the *Pators* were appointed to look after the administration of the *Elakas* in the hills section of the kingdom on behalf of the *Dolois*. But such practice was disallowed by the British and an order in the form of warning was issued to the effect that 'if a *Doloi* be compelled to be absent from his post for any length of time, the villagers, with the sanction of the Political Assistant Commissioner, should proceed to elect a *locum tenens*, who should possess and exercise the full powers of the absent *Doloi*. The proceedings and orders of an acting *Doloi* should have precisely the same force and effect as those of the permanently appointed *Doloi*, and should be open to revision only by the Principal Assistant Commissioner.[13] There was also a suggestion even to delimit the area of any *Elaka* if it is too extensive for one *Doloi* to efficiently perform his functions and the same be divided into two Doloiships.[14]

When a proposal for setting up of a school at Jowai came up, the question whether the *Dolois* and *Sirdars* had any knowledge of the three R's also arose. Therefore, an order was issued to the effect that 'no person should be eligible to the offices of *Doloi* and *Sirdar* who is unable to read and write both Bengali and Khasi languages.'[15] As far as this issue is concerned, G.D. Showers also made his comments and suggestions that, 'at present the *Dolois*, as regards letters, are as ignorant as the rest of the villagers. Arrangements should be introduced to encourage them to learn to read and write. For this purpose it might be ruled that, when a *Doloi* can record his own decisions, he should have higher powers conferred on him. These might be further extended from time to time till he is vested with the jurisdiction of a *Munsif* or *Sudder Ameen*.'[16] J.D. Gordon, had other ideas and plans as to the case of educating the *Dolois* in particular and the people in general. He was of the opinion that if the people had 'possessed a written language which the chief men among them could write and read, and which was known to the District Officer, or if they had been able to communicate with him directly, either in English or Bengali, instead of being obliged to approach him through an interpreter, he would not have been kept in ignorance either of their feelings or of their designs. If they had possessed even the elementary knowledge taught in the vernacular Schools of Bengal, they would have known the hopelessness of armed opposition to the government. To educate the Khasis and Jaintias, therefore, is a duty the discharge of which is forced upon the government as a means no less of governing these hills than of improving the condition of the people.'[17]

W.J. Allen and others pressed for the need in putting forward this condition that the *Dolois, Sirdars* and other chiefs should be able to read and write so that they may be in a position to converse with the British officials appointed in the area in a manner the British wanted it. Allen expressed his surprise 'how some of the *Dolois* and *Sirdars* who visited him were able to transact the commonest village duties at all' without being able to read and write. Perhaps to Allen it was a surprise of how these illiterate leaders of the society could transact business in administration. But this was because of Allen's ignorance of the traditional practice of administration and decision-making process and the convention followed and respected by the chiefs and the people since time immemorial in transacting their duties and decision reached at the *durbars* or councils. He should have known that the knowledge of three R' is not an important qualification at all than that of being well conversant with the traditional customs, laws and usages of the land.

In order to put more stringent control over the powers and functions of the *Dolois*, on many occasions, the British government on some flimsy grounds either asked the *Dolois* to tender or reject their resignation. Similarly, in some other cases, the *Dolois* were either fined or dismissed from their offices on the same flimsy grounds. The following few cases are worth mentioning as illustrations to prove such irrational actions taken by the British government.

Case No. I: In 1906-07, U Lajai, the *Doloi* of Nongphyllut, was convicted of illegally collecting subscriptions from his *raiyats* and fined Rs. 100. As a result, he tendered his resignation and an election was ordered to be held for the appointment of the successor.[18]

Case No. II: The *Doloi* of Nartiang in 1906-07 was fined Rs. 30 for neglecting to report an unnatural death in his village to the Sub-divisional Officer of the Jowai Subdivision.[19]

Case No. III: In 1906-07, U Khroo, the *Doloi* of Jowai, was three times fined for disobedience of orders.[20]

Case No. IV: In 1909, U Riangmaha, *Doloi* of Nongtalang, tendered his resignation owing to ill-health but it was not accepted, pending payment in full of the house tax from his circle.[21]

Case No. V: In 1911-12, the Subdivisional Officer of Jowai Subdivision forwarded a report of his not being satisfied with the performance of the *Dolois* of Bhoi and Nongtalang. The former has been very lax in paying up his revenue in due time. The latter neglected to do his duties and was called upon to show cause why he should not be dismissed.[22]

Case No. VI: In 1914-15, U Shui, who was officiating *Doloi* of Nongtalang, was removed from his office for the apathy he displayed in detecting the delinquents who looted a fishery in Sylhet district, which borders the Jaintia Hills. The *Langdoh* of Nongtalang was appointed to officiate as *Doloi* of the *Elaka*.[23]

Case No. VII: In 1914-15, U Long, *Doloi* of Satpator, tendered his resignation on the score of old age, but it was not accepted as the Subdivisional Officer of the Jaintia Hills Subdivison wanted him to collect his revenue before his successor was appointed.[24]

When the proposal came from C.K. Hudson, the Principal Assistant Commissioner, for the imposition of a house tax in Jaintia Hills, it was also suggested that the amount due from each *Elaka* should be collected exclusively through the agency of its own village authorities, that is, the *Dolois*, *Sirdars* and other village authorities. They were to receive a commission of 20 per cent on their collections. This similar system was pursued by the British in the Colehan in the South West Frontier Agency, where the

Mankees and Mondas were responsible for the collection of revenue of their respective villages.[25] With this new system introduced in Jaintia Hills, the traditional chiefs were made responsible for the collection of house tax and thus their status was reduced to that of "Commission Agents" of the British Government. They were therefore made to help raised the income and revenue of the alien Government by extracting the same from their own people.

Whether these changes made by the British were for the better or worse, the fact remains that the British administration had definitely upset the traditional political system operating in the land. For example, the British authority alone could approve the election of a *Doloi*, and he might be removed in case of proved misbehaviour either to the people or to the British. Therefore, under the alien government 'the democratic process that existed in Jaintia Hills in whatever dimension began to erode. Now the British authorities had become the absolute masters in Jaintia Hills with no other authority to limit their power over the Jaintias.'[26]

Though the British had retained the office of the *Doloi* along with that of the *Pator* and *Waheh Chnong*, most of their powers and functions were deprived of, curtailed and stripped of. Now they became the commission agents of the British, while retaining a semblance of civil and criminal jurisdiction over petty matters. But this act of curtailment the power of the traditional chiefs was rather a matter between the chiefs and the British authorities.

The fact that the Deputy Commissioner of the district had the power to approve the election of the *Doloi* also made it clear that the power over the chiefs had passed to the British authority. The people then respected the chief, not so much because they agreed that he should be the chief, but because of the fear of the authority which he derived from the British. So, there was a change in the power concept in Jaintia Hills with the coming of the British. But this change was not felt by the people, as they were ruled by their own chiefs, who belonged to their own tribe. So, as between the chiefs and the people, the former enjoyed more power than ever before, though that power was simply the radiation of the British power. In fact, in matters of precedence, the *Dolois* were raised from the third to the first rank. The chiefs were quite satisfied with the new power they received from the British and the people could not, under such circumstances, start any movement against the strong police system of the British.[27]

Restrictions on Civil and Criminal Powers of the Chiefs

The Khasi and Jaintia Hills after they have been taken over by the British, were constituted into a Political District, removed from the jurisdiction of the ordinary Criminal, and Revenue Courts, and of the offices established under the General Regulations and Acts. The administration of the country was vested in the Chief Commissioner of Assam, the Deputy Commissioner of the Khasi and Jaintia Hills and his Assistants, and the native Chiefs. The district was divided into three portions — namely, British possessions in the Khasi Hills, petty dependent and semi-dependent States in the Khasi Hills; and the Jaintia Hill country, which was wholly British. Thus the whole of Jaintia Hills along with few other villages in Khasi Hills were treated as 'British Areas'. These 'British Areas' were administered directly by the British authorities, while the Khasi States were granted internal autonomy subject to general control of the British Government.

In February 1835, Colonel Lister was appointed Political Agent in the Khasi Hills, with his headquarters at Nongkhlaw and the command of the sylhet Light Infantry battalion was also placed in his hands.[28] Thus, Lister who took charge on the 11th February 1835, became the first British Political Agent of the Khasi Hills Political Agency, with the charge of British relations with the Jaintia *Raja*.[29]

After the 15th of March 1835, the hills portion of Jaintia Hills was placed under the same Political Agency, that is, Khasi Hills, under the charge of Captain Lister. After his appointment as the Political Agent, Lister was also instructed to exercise magisterial functions in some villages, while the chiefs of others were permitted to retain entire jurisdiction within their own limits. As far as Jaintia Hills is concerned, 'initially', soon after the British took over the administration, the Political Agent permitted the *Dolois* and *Sirdars* to continue their traditional practice in investigating and deciding all civil suits wihout limitation, and all criminal cases not of a heinous nature.[30] Subsequently, however, the Political Agent reported that according to his view the people were not satisfied with the proceedings of their village chiefs. Therefore, he considered it necessary to place further restrictions on the civil and criminal powers of the *Dolois* and *Sirdars*. Accordingly, in 1841, he limited their jurisdiction in civil suits to the value of Rs. 50, and prohibited them from trying all criminal cases in which they, their relatives and dependants, and other chiefs were in any way concerned. Appeals from all orders and decisions of the *Dolois* and *Sirdars* in civil and criminal cases, were received and determined by the Political Agent and parties who choose to prefer their complaints, civil or criminal, direct to the Political Agent, were permitted to do so.[31]

The Political Agent enjoyed both civil and criminal powers in the district. He was empowered to fine to the extent of Rs. 500, and to imprison for two years on proceedings held before him as Magistrate, and, with the assistance of the *panchayat*, to imprison for five years. In respect of all cases of heinous nature, he was directed to send them to the *Sudder* court. He was further directed, as a general rule, to consider those villages under his jurisdiction "which have become ours by right of conquest, but that in those villages which have all along retained their independence or have been restored by us to their former Chiefs", to exercise only political control.[32] In those cases of a civil nature, the *Sudder* court was empowered, on an inspection of the Agent's periodical returns or on a petition being presented to it, to call for and revise his proceedings. At the same time, Harry Inglis was appointed to be an assistant to Lister with full powers to punish to the extent of one year's imprisonment and Rs. 200 fine, his proceedings being always subject to the revision of the Political Agent.[33]

In order to cover other areas under the civil and criminal powers and the jurisdiction of the Political Agent, Act VI of 1835 was passed by the British authorities. Thus as per this Act, 'the Political Agent of the Khasi Hills was placed in civil and criminal cases under the control and superintendence of the *Sudder Dewanny* and *Nizamut Adawlut*, respectively and on a reference from the court, the Government, by their orders No. 193 of the 29th of September 1835, authorised the extension of the court's jurisdiction to the Jaintia territory.'[34] This action was taken with the assumption by the court that Jaintia Hills formed part of the Khasi territory and conceived that, under the provision of Act VI of 1835, they were competent to excercise authority therein. However, Jaintia Hills formed no part of the Khasi territories, and the said Act could have no possible application to it.[35] The reason being that as A.J.M. Mills opined, "we were not in possession of the Jaintia country when the Act was passed."[36] Subsequently, the British Government sanctioned, under Act XXXI of 1836, the general annexation of the Jaintia territories to Sylhet, and the extension to it of the laws and regulations, but the plain country on this side of the hills to Sylhet was only brought under the operation of this order.[37]

There were some problems which developed in the case of Jaintia Hills as to the enforcement and extension of Act VI of 1835 over the area. The reason as opined by A.J.M. Mills being that "the Jaintia Hills cannot be constituted a part of the Khasi Hills. The territories are distinct, and the Assistant to the Agent cannot, legally exercise the powers which he now does in the Jaintia Hills."[38] For this reason, it was quite clear that Mills was not in favour of the extension of the same Act both over Khasi and Jaintia Hills as the latter area is distinctly different as per his observations "Jaintia is at present placed in a very anomalous position. The regulations, though ordered to be extended to it, have not been so extended, while the order for extending the jurisdiction of the *Sudder Dewanny* and *Nizamut Adawluts* under Act VI of 1835 to the territory, though carried into effect, was clearly founded on wrong premises. It is desirable that these anomalies regarding jurisdiction should be removed."[39] But then as to the rules by which justice was administered, Lister stated that,

> "he is guided in exercising control over the Khasi and Jaintia Hills by the spirit of the instructions of Government and by the Assam rules. The instructions themselves are of a very vague character, and the Assam rules have been extended to this country without any authority whatever . . .; and further the rules forwarded are those which have not yet received the confirmation of Government and have therefore not been introduced into Assam."[40]

The Political Agent, Mr. Lister, having faced with those problems in the administration of justice, made certain suggestions for further implementation of other schemes to tone up the adminstration and the British interest in the area. To this effect, Lister suggested 'the enactment of a complete set of rules and procedures suited to the usages and institutions of the country.'[41]

Still, for further implementation of this end in view, he made another suggestion that 'a careful inquiry be made into the customs, habits, and institutions of the Jaintia territory.'[42] At the same time, he opined that,

> "if it be found, as asserted by Mr. Lewis, that the present mode in which petty cases are decided by the village authorities is the cause of vexation and annoyance to the people, and that cruel ordeals are still enforced, the procedure should be reformed, the mode in which cases are to be tried should be defined, and the powers of the *Dolois* should be indicated with precision. The country is ours, and it is our duty to see that speedy justice, suited to the simple habits of the people, is administered, and practices abhorent to humanity are not allowed."[43]

It is therefore very clear that, one of the major effects of the British administration on the traditional institutions in Jaintia Hills after its annexation was on the civil and criminal powers and functions of the traditional Chiefs who were responsible to dispense and conduct the administration of justice over the people of their area. This is because in the pre-British period, civil and criminal powers were enjoyed by the *Dolois, Pators* and village headmen of each village. While dispensing justice, a Chief acted as a judge and the *durbar* or council as the jury. In this case it is always the combination of both these institutions. The traditional system of administration of justice is also confined to the judicial system prevailing today on the patterns devised by traditional rulers in the past. The traditional judicial institution of the Jaintias was continued by the British with slight modifications.[44]

After the British annexed Jaintia Hills in 1835, they introduced many changes and put forward a number of restrictions on the powers and functions of the traditional institutions. Some of these changes and restrictions were drastic in nature which in the long run had serious and tremendous effects on the civil and criminal powers of the *Dolois* and other traditional Chiefs. The traditional Chiefs who were also the leaders of their people, enjoyed enormous power and functions, though circumscribed, as entrusted to them by the people on the basis of traditions, customs and usages before the coming of the British into the scene. Besides the *Dolois*, there were also under them other traditional Chiefs like the *Langdoh* (priest), *Pator* and village headmen. These Chiefs were also responsible within their jurisdiction to investigate and try cases of civil and criminal nature. The suits were to come first before the priest, with an appeal to the *Pator*, and from him, if not satisfactory, to the *Dolois*. The *Pators* can hear cases in *durbar* and act for their principals, the *Dolois*, during the latter's absence or illness. In those *Elakas* where the office of *Pator* did not exist, the *Dolois* transacted all business themselves. Moreover, it was found according to Allen's report that,

> "In villages at a distance from the place of residence of the *Doloi*, almost all preliminary inquiries are made, and all petty civil and criminal cases are first heard and frequently settled by the *Langdohs* in *durbar*. If the decision of the *Langdoh* does not give satisfaction, the case is brought before the *Doloi*, or, if he happens to be absent, before his deputy, the *Pator*. If the *Pator* decides the case, either party may have it reheard by the *Doloi* on his return to the village, and a third decision is then made by the *Doloi* in *durbar*. If the *Doloi's* judgement be not approved of, the case is carried before the Principal Assistant Commissioner at Cherrapunji."[45]

Parallel to the coersive measures to subdue the resistance of the Khasis and Jaintias against the British authorities, the Government of Bengal had taken steps to constitute a system of administration to bring these tribes gradually under their effective control. The task of framing the system may be said to have been commenced since the suppression of the Khasi insurrection and in particular after the annexation of the Jaintia Hills in 1835. From the outset, it was realised that the problems of governing a hill tribe were distinct from those of the plains. For the hillmen had never acknowledged the authority of any foreigners and they were, as General Showers later observed, "in the rudest state" of civilization. Mindful of the uniqueness of the problem in the hills, the Government set up a separate Political Agency of the Khasi Hills in which the Jaintia Hills was also included later after its annexation.[46]

The chief authority of the Khasi and Jaintia Hills territory, whether designated as the Political Agent or the Principal Assistant to the Commissioner, had to perform dual functions as the

Civil Magistrate and the Political Agent. In Jaintia Hills, the British had, however, absolute jurisdiction as it was their conquered territory. In the case of these hills as well, the Government followed a cautious policy. Lister had, however, endeavoured to bring the Jaintias under the authority of the Government.[47]

With regard to the existing judicial power held by the *Dolois* of adjudicating petty and criminal suits, Morton felt that this power should be withdrawn from them and suitors referred directly to the Assistant Commissioner at Raliang. By doing so, Morton was of the opinion that the people of Jaintia Hills would then be taught to look to the Government office for justice. The Assistant Commissioner should, he thought, hold the powers of a First Class Subordinate Magistrate and *Sudder Ameen*. The hillmen should be encouraged to refer their suits to arbitration; the arbitrators, however, șitting in the presence of the Assistant.[48] Morton, further favoured the idea of giving more judicial power to the Assistant Commissioner in the area so that its people would always seek justice from the officers of the Government and not their traditional Chiefs or institutions as used to be a practice.[49] Moreover, to enhance the judicial power of the British officials, "mere village arbitration should not be accepted as decisive of a suit, though the circumstance of parties having agreed to abide by the verdict of one or more arbitration, should, as in Assam, be admitted in evidence."[50] But in the case of Jaintia Hills, "no agents or counsel, under any pretence, should be admitted in the Jaintia Court", was Morton's opinion.[51]

In respect of the court proceedings, Morton agreed with Allen's recommendation that they should be conducted in the simplest manner, except in heinous cases, and the entire record being in the Assistant's own handwriting. The proceedings in heinous cases, not exceeding the powers of the Deputy Commissioner, should be taken down by the Assistant in English and forwarded for orders, it remaining optional with the Deputy Commissioner to summon the parties to his court. Other heinous cases should, of course, be heard by the Deputy Commissioner himself in the usual manner. All appeals, civil and criminal, from the order of the Assistant Commissioner should lie to the Deputy Commissioner at Shillong.[52]

The above drastic measures if implemented as suggested by Morton, would actually reduced the judicial power, so far empowered to the *Dolois*, to nothing but mere silent spectators of the enhanced power and authority of the Assistant Commissioner and other officials above him. The traditional judicial powers of the *Dolois* were already taken away from them but left with power to adjudicate only over petty cases. Over and above this, Morton's idea was to strip them of completely even those petty cases which were earlier granted to the *Dolois*.

The various changes introduced by the British in the area, had the same effects on the other traditional offices and institutions — like that of the *Pator* and *Langdoh*, besides the *Doloi's*. With regard to the office of *Pator*, there was a time when a recommendation was made for its abolition. Allen was the man behind this idea. In his report, he recommended that as the first step towards a reform in the administration of public affairs in the fifteen Doloiships should be to abolish the office of Pator.[53] However, Showers did not agree to this. He gave these reasons in favour of retaining the office of *Pator*. Firstly, according to Showers, the *Pator* was simply the assistant to the *Doloi*, and exercised no independent power. Secondly, there were occasions when the *Doloi* was obliged to leave the village to meet, for instance, the Commissioner or Deputy Commissioner, and when he supplied a large number of coolies, he accompanied the party that employed them. At such time an acting *Doloi* will be wanted, and the *Pator* would be fitter to perform the duties than a person elected for the time. Inconvenience might attend the appointment of one who was to hold it but for a time and who might be opposed to the *Doloi*.[54] In the subsequent development, Showers' idea of retaining the *Pator's* office remained unchanged; the office continued to exist till today in Jaintia Hills.

With regard to the office of *Langdoh* or village priest, 'he was indeed the first ruler of a village whose office was elective. In the beginning, he combined in himself both the sacerdotal and secular functions. In course of time, with the increase of political functions, the office of *U Waheh Chnong* (village headman) was created.'[55] After the creation of the office of *U Waheh Chnong*, the *Langdoh* was put incharge only over those religious matters. In the days goneby, the *Langdoh* played an important role in the administration and decision-making process, even to the extent of presiding over the destiny of the Jaintia rulers. However, it may thus be stated that:

> "no category of rulers in *Ri Jaintia*, be he a *Raja*, a *Doloi*, a *Pator* or a *Waheh Chnong*, could become oppressive beyond a certain limit for fear of being removed from their post by the people. Nor could the people take the law into their own hands since they should have the recommendation of the priest. Hence, the priest appeared to be the ultimate reservior of power in *Ri Jaintia*. However, the priest could not simply submit to any popular demand unless it was sanctioned by apparent divine authority as interpreted by him."[56]

We found the office of *Langdoh* having continued even during the British period of administration, but he was without any political power or role. It was reported that during the British period, in large villages, where the *Doloi* did nor reside, the *Langdoh* exercised judicial authority in minor cases. A certain British official, Showers, wanted that the *Langdoh's* office and their authority be continued. He also suggested that the *Langdoh* might be required to act as the superior police officer in the village, and to send his reports by the *Sangot* or other village *Peadah* to the *Doloi*.[57] Unfortunately, 'under the British, like that of the institution of kingship, the second institution to go was that of the priest. The British had deprived him of his political role in presiding over the destiny of Jaintia rulers. His role was then confined purely to religious matters. Whatever secular functions that had been enjoyed by the priest had been completely taken over by the British.'[58]

The simple procedures adopted by the traditional Chiefs relating to the trial of civil and criminal cases were made more complicated by the British authorities after they have introduced those innumerable changes. Through these changes, not only that the powers and functions of the Chiefs were taken away or stripped off, from adjudicating the cases of serious and heinous nature, but the cases brought forward and tried by the British officials had to pass through different stages before they were finally decided by the authorities concerned. The system was not only complicated but time consuming and thus created hazardous hurdles which led to dissatisfaction among the people.

The implementation and enforcement of the various changes as suggested and introduced from time to time by the British officials serving in the area, ultimately led to affect drastically the traditional role and functions of the Chiefs in Jaintia Hills. In this way, the authoritative role of the Chiefs was curtailed to a great extent. This process appeared very clearly in the new role played by an European Officer that when he be appointed, he was entrusted with the power to see that "the judicial powers of the village authorities should be gradually curtailed, and they should be employed only in deciding the pettiest civil and criminal cases on police duties, and as assessors or jurymen in cases in which their assistants would be useful to the Sub-Assistant Commissioner."[59] Moreover, it may be added that in Allen's opinion, the "resources of the Jaintia Hills will not be efficiently developed, neither will the people obtain what can be properly called justice, till a European Officer is stationed in their hills."[60]

With such tremendous powers vested in the hands of the British officers, the traditional Chiefs in the area were reduced to mere assessors or jurymen and can decide the least of the cases referred to them. Over and above that, they were placed entirely in the hands and under the overall control of the British Sub-Assistant Commissioner stationed in the area. The same mode and procedure adopted in the Santhal Parganahs of the tribal areas of Chotanagpur was brought and applied in Jaintia Hills too, which in Allen's own words, "in all probability would be found suitable to these rude and ignorant mountaineers."[61]

REFERENCES

1. Pakem, B. 'The Socio-political System of the Jaintia Tribe of Assam: An Analysis of Continuity and Change', in K. Suresh Singh (Ed.). *Tribal Situation in India*, IIAS, Simla 1972, p. 353.
2. Allen, W.J. *Report on the Administration of the Cossyah and Jynteah Hill Territory*, 1858, Shillong 1975 (Reprint), p. 72.
3. Mackenzie, A. *The North-East Frontier of India*, Delhi 1979 (Reprint), p. 239.
4. Pakem, B. *op. cit.*
5. Allen, W.J. *op. cit.*, p. 66.
6. *Ibid.*
7. *Ibid.*, p. 23.
8. *Ibid.*, p. 66
9. *Selections from the Records of the Government of Bengal* No. XXXIX, Pat I. Papers relating to the disturbances in the Cossyah and Jynteah Hills, Calcutta,

1863 (hereafter *Selections from Records*); Showers to Secretary Govt. of Bengal, 9th June 1862, p. 165.
10. *Ibid.*, Morton to Major Agnew, 9th July 1862, p. 219.
11. Allen, W.J. *op. cit.*, pp. 69–70.
12. *Ibid.*, p. 68.
13. *Ibid.*
14. *Ibid.*
15. *Ibid.*, p. 73.
16. *Selections from Records, op. cit.*
17. *Ibid.*, Gordon to Haughton, No. 436, 8th September 1862, pp. 240–241.
18. *Annual Report on the Administration of the Khasi and Jaintia HIlls for the year* 1906–07, (hereafter *Annual Administration Report*) No. 802, Shillong 8th May 1907; F.E. Jackson to the Commissioner, Surma Valley and Hill Districts, p. 5.
19. *Ibid.*
20. *Annual Administration Report* for the year ending 31st March 1909; Shillong 12th May 1900; L.O. Clarke to the Commissioner Surma Valley and Hill Districts, Sichar, p. 5.
21. *Ibid.*, p. 6.
22. *Annual Administration Report* for the year 1911-12; No. 3062, Silchar 6th July 1912, Commissioner Surma Valley and Hill Districts to the Chief Secy., Chief Commissioner of Assam, p. 6.
23. *Annual Administration Report* for the year 1914-15; No. 2106, Shillong 28th May 1915, A.W. Dentith to the Commissioner Surma Valley and HIlls Districts, p. 8.
24. *Ibid.*
25. Allen, W.J. *op. cit.*, p. 72.
26. Pakem, B. 'The Changing Structure of the Political Institution of Jaintia Chieftainship', *NEICSSR Journal*, Shillong, Vol. I, No. I April 1977, p. 2.
27. Pakem, B. *op. cit.*, 354–355.
28. Hunter, W.W. *A Statistical Account of Assam*, Vol. II (1879), B.R. Publishing Corporation (Reprint), Delhi 1975, pp. 203–204, 206.
29. Mills, A.J.M. *op. cit.* p. 1.
30. Allen, W.J. *op. cit.*, p. 66.
31. *Ibid.* see also A.J.M. Mills, *op. cit.*, p. 4.
32. Mills, A.J.M. *op cit.*, p. 8.
33. *Ibid.*
34. *Ibid.*, pp. 8–9.
35. *Ibid.*, p. 9.
36. *Ibid.*
37. *Ibid.*
38. *Ibid.*
39. *Ibid.*, pp. 9–10.
40. *Ibid.*, p. 10.
41. *Ibid.*, p. 11.
42. *Ibid.*
43. *Ibid.*
44. Pakem, B. 'Administration of Justice in Jaintia HIlls', in S.K. Chattopadhyaya (Ed). *Tribal Institutions of Meghalaya*, Spectrum Publications, Guwahati 1985, p. 173.

45. Allen, W.J. *op. cit.*, p. 67.
46. Dutta, P.N. *Impact of the West on the Khasis and Jaintias*, Cosmo Publications, New Delhi 1982, p. 102.
47. *Ibid.*, pp. 103–104.
48. *Selections from Records, op. cit.* Morton to Agnew, 9th July 1862, p. 219.
49. *Ibid.*
50. *Ibid.*, p. 219.
51. *Ibid.*
52. *Ibid.*
53. Allen, W.J. *op. cit.*, p. 67.
54. *Selections from Records, op. cit.* Showers to the Secretary Government of Bengal, 9th June 1862, pp. 166–167.
55. Pakem, B. *NEHU Journal, op. cit.*, p. 50.
56. Pakem, B.: *NEICSSR Journal, op. cit.*, p. 2.
57. *Selections from Records, op. cit.* Showers to the Secretary Government of Bengal, 9th June 1862, p. 167.
58. Pakem, B. *op. cit.*
59. Allen, W.J. *op. cit.*, p. 69.
60. *Ibid.*
61. *Ibid.*

CHAPTER V

District Council: Its Effects on Traditional Institutions and Leadership

The Khasi-Jaintia society had its deep-rooted tribal institutions since time immemorial. However, these pristine institutions had to face severe stress and strains at the oncoming forces of new administrative set up and modernisation processes in the field of constitutional administration. With the advent and evolution of such agents of political modernisation and the emergence of the new institutions in the area, many changes had taken place. These changes had brought immense effects on the power and functions of the traditional institutions and the traditional Chiefs. This has also certainly created a changing role and power-relationship between the two sets of institutions. While the traditional institutions have been operating in the traditional socio-political structure, standing for the old traditional values and institutions and satisfying various traditional needs of the tradition-oriented society, the newly created constitutional institutions stand for and committed to economic, social and political change and modernisation. As such, the new political institutions which were created after Independence were in fact eroding the powers and functions of traditional councils instead of improving upon them.[1] The immediate effect was that the powers and functions of these traditional institutions were taken away and they were put under the overall control and supervision of the District Council. This was another blow which had actually first started during the Colonial administration on the part of those institutions and Chiefs who had the privilege of serving and supervising the administration of their own people according to the traditional customs and usages of the land.

While majority of the traditional institutions were retained by the British authorities, their powers were greatly reduced. For example, the British had done away with the political role of the priest in presiding over the destiny of Jaintia rulers. His role was then confined purely to religious matters.[2] In other words, 'the divine' authority. They concentrated more political power in the hands of the secular authorities. The secular authorities had ultimately become the tools of the British. When the British authority was removed in 1947, the power of the secular authorities was drastically reduced and the District Councils assumed power over them.[3] The power and functions of such secular traditional institutions were therefore further curtailed and reduced by the District Council under the Sixth Schedule to the Constitution of India. The effects of the District Council on these traditional institutions and Chiefs were tremendous. However, being a democratic political institution, the District Council used to be at logger heads with the traditional authorities.[4]

In the case of the village *durbars* (councils), the Census Report of 1961 remarked that, 'the present powers of the *durbar* under the District Council has greatly been reduced in comparison with its powers under the Chiefs.'[5] If the District Council could interfere in the village affairs, it was more so in the case of the *Durbar Raids*.[6] The Census Report was again very clear on this point when it added that, 'the part of the *Durbar Raid* is played by the District Council.'[7] Precisely because of this fact, 'the *Dolois* in Jaintia Hills were under the control of the District Council. But most of the *Dolois* did not like to part with the power which they had enjoyed under the British, and some even treated the District Council with disdain.'[8]

Many other changes had taken place in the traditional Chiefs — District Council relationship since independence. During the transitional period, there had been a change from tradition to modernity. The Pataskar Commission has rightly observed that,

> One of the purposes of the Sixth Schedule was to allow the tribal people to administer themselves in all matters of vital local concern and to save them from an administration that was both expensive and remote. The tendency of the Councils has, on the other hand, been to substitute this traditional system of administration by something far more alien to the

full-fledged democratic apparatus of Government elsewhere.[9]

The process of change could be clearly noticed in the case of the traditional Chiefs in Jaintia Hills of Meghalaya. The District Council appears not only to be far more alien to the traditional institutions, but the powers and functions of the traditional Chiefs had been threatened due to its existence in the area. Because of this reason, the District Council was never welcomed by the traditional Chiefs. It may further be noted that,

> The District Council under the Sixth Schedule had replaced the British and Indian administrative system over tribal affairs in *Ri Jaintia*. But the stepping of the District Council into the shoes of either the Jaintia Raja or the British and Indian authorities did not bring any improvement in the power position of the Chiefs. On the contrary, the new power structure had radically reduced the powers of the Chiefs.[10]

The United Khasi-Jaintia Hills Autonomous District Council which was established in 1952, passed a number of Acts, Rules and Regulations from time to time. Some of these Acts had a direct bearing and tremendous effect on the powers and functions of the traditional institutions and Chiefs in the area. We now examine some of these Acts which have such direct effects on the Chiefs.

The traditional Chiefs in Jaintia Hills — the *Dolois, Pators, Sirdars* and village headmen are now treated by the District Council as its subordinate officials. These Chiefs are therefore completely under the control and supervision of the District Council. This could be made effective on the basis of certain provisions that contained in the Sixth Schedule. For example, under the provision of paragraph 3(1) (g) of the Sixth Schedule, the District Council is empowered to make laws with respect to — "the appointment or succession of Chiefs or Headmen". A specific example to this effect may be mentioned here in detail to that of Khasi and Jaintia Hills.

The United Khasi-Jaintia Hills Autonomous District Council passed an Act (Act No. II of 1959), known as the United Khasi-Jaintia Hills Autonomous District (Appointment and Succession of Chiefs and Headmen) Act, 1959 (hereinafter referred to as the Principal Act) on the 21st October 1959, after receiving the assent of the Governor of Assam on the 16th October 1959. This Act made provisions for the election and appointment of Chiefs and headmen, confirmation of Chiefs, dispute regarding election of Chiefs etc.

In brief, all appointments of Chiefs shall be subject to the approval of the District Council which may confirm such appointments under terms and conditions which it may by Rules from time to time adopt. Such terms and conditions shall, among others provide for:

(a) the duration of their office,
(b) their remuneration,
(c) their relationship with the District Council and/or with the *Elaka*,
(d) the manner in which the administration of the *Elaka* will be carried out by them,
(e) the manner in which the fund of the *Elaka* is to be managed by them,
(f) their code of conduct;

Provided that pending the adoption of such terms and conditions the existing terms and conditions under which the existing Chiefs were appointed shall continue to be in force.

Provided further that the terms and conditions that may be adopted by the District Council under this Section shall immediately apply to all the existing Chiefs.

Regarding dispute of election of Chiefs, the Act clearly states that,

> If any dispute arises regarding any matter relating to, or connected with, the election of Chief, the dispute shall within 30 days after the publication of the result of the election be referred by the party or parties concerned to the Executive Committee for decision. An appeal against the decision of the Executive Committee shall lie to a tribunal constituted for the purpose by the district council and the decision of the tribunal shall be final. Any appeal before the tribunal shall be filed within 30 days after the order of the Executive Committee is communicated to the party or parties concerned.

Besides this, the Act also made provision for the removal and suspension of the Chiefs and Headmen by the Executive

Committee of the District Council if in its opinion these incumbents violated the following terms and conditions of their appointment:

a) he (the Chief/Headmen) violates any of the terms and condition of his appointment; refuses to carry out the instructions issued by the Executive Committee; violates any of the law, regulations, rules and the resolutions passed by the District Council or any customary rights and practices, oppresses his people or misrules his *Elaka;*
b) he has lost the confidence of the majority of the people of his *Elaka;*
c) he is found to be mentally unfit to carry out his functions or becomes a criminal or an insolvent;
d) he is conducting himself in a manner derogatory to his office or prejudicial to the interest of his *Elaka* or any part thereof, or which may undermine the authority of the District Council.

Provided that every such case shall be placed before the District Council at its next session.

Provided further that no Chief shall be removed from office unless he is given an opportunity of being heard.

The amendment to the Principal Act of 1959 made by the Act No. I of 1959 and the Act No. II of 1971 has further added the following terms and conditions relating to the manner of removal and suspension of Chiefs:

The Chief may be removed from office or suspended by the Executive Committee of the District Council if in its opinion:

i) he has been incapable of carrying on the administration to the satisfaction of the Executive Committee due to ill-health, old age or habitual drunkeness; or
ii) he violates any customary rights and practices prevailing in the *Elaka* concerned and duly approved by the Executive Committee; or
iii) he has been convicted of an offence involving moral turpitude; or
iv) has been [sic] oppressed the people of the *Elaka* and they have just cause for dissatisfaction with his misrule;
v) he has lost the confidence of the majority of his electors or of the people of the *Elaka;*

vi) he is an undischarged insolvent; or
vii) he does not reside in the *Elaka*.

The United Khasi-Jaintia Hills Autonomous District Council in the aforesaid Act (Principal Act of 1959) introduced two fundamental changes from the traditional customary practices of the people as per Sections 10 and 11 of the Act which relate to the appointment of Deputy Chief (Section 10) and an Acting Chief (Section 11).

The Jaintia Hills Autonomous District Council which was established in 1964, adopted the Principal Act as it is during its initial years of existence. In the subsequent years, it made certain amendments to the Principal Act. For example, this District Council passed an amendment Act in 1973 (the Jaintia HIlls Act No. I of 1973) which deleted the entire Section 10 of the Principal Act of 1959 relating to the appointment of Deputy Chief. The Jaintia Hills Autonomous District Council realised the uselessness and inapplicability of such a provision of the Act in the area and more importantly it shows the complete deviation from the traditional customary practices of the people of Jaintia Hills. However, the Executive Committee of the Jaintia Hills District Council still retained Section 11 of the Principal Act relating to the appointment of an Acting Chief. This particular Section (Section 11) of the Principal Act of 1959 clearly stated that,

> If at any time the post of a Chief is vacant, the Executive Committee may by an order in writing appoint *any person* (emphasis ours) to act as an Acting Chief who will exercise all the power and functions of the Chief. An Acting Chief will remain in office until the appointment of a new Chief or until he is removed by the Executive Committee.

The Executive Committee of the District Council having armed with this constitutional power, appointed many such Acting Chiefs, especially *Dolois* in Jaintia Hills, either after the death, removal or suspension of the regular *Doloi* in an *Elaka*. Many such cases of appointment of Acting *Dolois* took place from time to time in several *Elakas* of Jaintia Hills District.

However, such an act of appointment of an Acting Chief has been criticised as it tantamounts to complete deviation from the traditional customary practice of the people. In this respect, a comment was made that, 'there was never a customary practice of appointing an Acting Chief. A Chief once appointed, he held the office for life, unless removed for very strong reasons, like moral turpitude or commission or heinous crimes.'[11] Moreover, according to the traditional customary practices, a Chief must be a person belonging to the particular clan or clans chosen from time immemorial. But the Act does not honour or take into cognisance the age-old tradition of the society. It may thus be noted that according to the aforesaid Section (Section 11) of the Principal Act, it mentioned very specifically that the Executive Committee of the District Council may appoint "any person" who could be from any clan to act as an Acting Chief and exercise all the power and functions of the Chief. This step taken by the District Council is sure to create confusion in the minds of the people. It also shows a complete deviation from the traditional practices and against the norms of the society.

In certain *Elakas* in Jaintia Hills, a *Doloi* of an *Elaka* receives as remuneration for the services rendered by him the *Rek* land or Service land, which means a revenue free land, for cultivation. Besides this, *Puja* land, also a revenue free land, is held and cultivated by a Chief or headman and the yield or income therefrom is utilised for meeting expenses connected with religious performances according to customs of each *Elaka*. But in the second amendment Act of 1975, the Jaintia Hills Autonomous District (Appointment and Succession of Chiefs and Headmen), Second Amendment Act 1975, inserted a new Section (Section 10) in the Principal Act of 1959, forfeiting the right to cultivate and enjoy *Services* and *Puja* lands by a Chief or headman who has been suspended or removed from office. This relevant Section (Section 10) of the amended Act stated clearly as follows:

> A Chief or Headman who has been suspended or removed from office under Section 6 or 9 shall and shall be deemed to have no longer any right to use and cultivate the Service or *Puja* lands and such lands shall revert and shall be deemed to have reverted to the District Council with effect from the date a Chief or Headman was suspended or removed from office and the District Council may either lease it out in any manner it deems fit and proper or keep it through its representatives or agent until a Chief or Headman is appointed:

> Provided that in case of any Service or *Puja* lands in which the Chief or Headman so removed or suspended had actually prepared such lands for the purpose of cultivation or has incurred expenditure on this account, the same may be allowed to be cultivated by him till the crops growing on the lands have been completely harvested and the Acting Chief or Headman shall be entitled to the benefit of such Service or *Puja* lands only at the close of such harvesting season.
>
> Provided further that in case where no Acting Chief or Headman has been appointed or when the office of a Chief or Headman falls vacant or remains unfilled, for reasons to be recorded in writing, the Executive Committee shall farm out for purpose of cultivation such service or *Puja* lands to any person through its authorised officer for such fixed sum and period of time or season as the Executive Committee may determine and such sum shall be credited to the fund of the Council.

Traditionally, the Service and *Puja* lands were primarily meant for the upkeep of chiefs and headmen and to meet such other expenses connected with religious performances. These plots were in the past specifically allotted to the chiefs and headmen by the *Syiem* and later on by the community. Thus according to traditional custom, in the absence of any chief either due to his death or removal from office by the people, such lands allotted to the chiefs will revert back to the community until a new chief is elected by the people. Until such time these lands will be looked after by the members of the chief's clan or clans. It was found that during the British rule, this customary practice of the people was allowed to continue and the alien rulers never interfered in the matter of the management of these lands. However, the situation is otherwise now under the District Council. A complete reverse development has taken place since the passing of the above mentioned Act by the District Council. Through this Act, the District Council is trying to appropriate land and its produce, which actually belongs to the *Elaka*. Thus, instead of acting as an institution to protect and preserve the traditions and social customs of the people, the District Council behaves otherwise and contrary to the purpose of its establishment in the area. This shows very clearly that the District Council unnecessarily tries to interfere in matters which should have been left to the people and to allow them to function independently in such area so that there is continuity of the traditional customs and practices. This is another glaring example of an effect of the modern political institution on such traditional institution. Such action on the part of the District Council gives rise to ill-feeling and conflicting relationship between the traditional and modern institutions.

It may also be stated that the Khasi Hills Autonomous District Council in 1980, in its Fifth amendment to the Principal Act of 1959, went even to the extent of passing an Act debarring the Chiefs, Deputy Chiefs and Acting Chiefs taking part in politics and elections either to the Parliament or the State Legislative Assembly or the District Council. To this effect, so far, the Jaintia Hills Autonomous District Council has not taken any cue from the Khasi Hills District Council in respect of debarring the Chiefs and headmen in Jaintia Hills from taking part in politics and election. Though the chiefs and headmen in the area are treated by the District Council as its subordinate officials, no such Act was introduced. Unlike that of Khasi Hills, and in the absence of any Act to debar them, the *Dolois, Pators,* and headmen in Jaintia Hills openly took part in electoral and party politics. We came across such cases that *Dolois* even hold important offices in a political party and openly presided over party meetings and campaigns during elections.

The chiefs being treated by the District Council as its subordinate officials, are made accountable for their actions to the District Council. They are therefore directed to desist from criticism of the functioning of the Executive Committee of the District Council in any form of utterance or statement. They are debarred to participate in any demonstration or resort to any form of strike in connection with any matter pertaining to their conditions of service. These conditions laid down by the District Council gave rise to the tussle with the traditional chiefs. Thus, 'the tussle between the traditional leader and the modern political elite is a continuing affair. On a slight pretext, the traditional Chief would be suspended on charges like insubordination, malpractices and disobedience.'[12]

The various Acts enforced by the District Council under the Sixth Schedule from time to time, brought radical changes in the patterns and procedure of election and appointment or succession of chiefs and headmen in the area under study. The effects of such Acts under the modern democratic set up on the traditional Chiefs resulted in reducing and subordinating their position and status to that of 'stipendiary official. It was not so in the olden days, not even during the British regime.'[13] The District Council even considered the chiefs as its 'administrative heads, and the (State) Government was advised to direct Heads of Departments not to correspond with them directly.'[14] Such scheme of action on the part of the District Council obviously created much resentment among the traditional institutions in their relationship and dealing with the District Council. Thus the District Council was 'never welcome to the traditional authorities in the hills as to them it reflected the aspirations of the new elite. In all other Autonomous Districts (except the then Mizo District) compromises were made with the traditional institutions and everywhere they failed in a general way. This created problems in all the Hills districts where public awareness was high enough to generate resentment.'[15]

Thus, under the new constitutional set up, the chiefs are pushed behind the line of leadership. They are to keep themselves content with whatever power and functions left to them by the District Council. Though the District Council granted certain unofficials pickings to the Chiefs, it reduced them to a much lesser officials. In the District Council's dealing with the chiefs, there is a strong feeling that it has not fully appreciated their continuance as institutions of the best in their traditions and has therefore been dealing with them as personalities or individuals of their respective *Himas* or *Elakas*. This naturally leads to indefinite policy of preserving the institutions in their pristine purity. This has caused a sense of confusion among the people in general, a feeling of uncertainty, if not of mistrust or suspicion among the Chiefs of the motive of the District Council as to their continuance as custodians and trustees of the customs and traditions of the people.[16] As of now, the absence of any association among the *Dolois* and other village authorities in Jaintia Hills to act as pressure group or lobby in order to assert their grievances or even their feelings about the functioning of the District Council, makes their position very weak and ineffective. They have therefore to accept whatever policy decisions taken by the District Council in their relationship with it. On the other hand, the District Council has taken advantage of the situation and passed many such Acts in its favour which are at the same time binding on the chiefs to act in accordance with the Council's prerogative. The District Council has thus become 'an authority to control the *Dolois;* and at the same time, an integrative agency for the different *Doloiships*. In a sense, it is not far away from becoming a centralised authority. The *Dolois* are now completely under the control of the District Council, though they were not so much used to the system of control when they were nominally under the Jaintia Rajas.'[17]

The relationship between the traditional institutions and that of the District Council was all along under strains. Paradoxically, the present situation is a threat to the traditional institutions as well as to whatever democratic practices practiced by the people of the area under study. There existed, therefore, drastic effects on the power, functions and leadership role of the traditional chiefs with the coming into existence of the District Council. Further, under such a precarious situation, frontal leadership in the area or for that matter in the whole State of Meghalaya passed into the hands of the emerging elite. The prevailing condition appears to be more in favour of such elite than the old guards of tradition.

REFERENCES

1. Pakem, B. "Political Development and Change in North East India", in *Changing North-East India* (Ed.), A.P. Sinha, Gagan Publishers, Ludhiana 1986, p. 35.
2. Pakem, B. *NEICSSR Journal, op. cit.*, p. 2.
3. Pakem, B. "Political Development and Change in North-East India", *op. cit.*, pp. 44–45.
4. *Ibid.*, p. 45
5. *Census Reports of India*, 1961, Vol. III, Part VI, No. 13, p. 46.
6. Pakem, B. "The Socio-Political System of the Jaintia Tribe of Assam: An Analysis of Continuity and Change," *op. cit.*, p. 355.
7. *Census-Reports of India*, 1961, *op. cit.*, p. 47.
8. Pakem, B. "The Socio-Political System of the Jaintia Tribe of Assam: An Analysis of Continuity and Change", *op cit.*
9. *Report of the Commission on the Hill Areas of Assam 1965-66* (Pataskar Commission), Delhi 1966, p. 65.
10. Pakem, B. *NEICSSR Journal, op. cit.*, p. 3.
11. *Report of the Land Reforms Commission for Khasi Hills*, Shillong 1974, p. 8.
12. Pakem, B. "Meghalaya: Some Aspects of Political Development", in *North-East India: A Sociological Study*, (Ed.) S.M. Dubey, Concept Publishing Company, Delhi 1978, p. 236.

13. *Report of the Land Reforms Commission for Khasi Hills,* Shillong 1974, p. 8.
14. *Report of the Land Reforms Commission for Khasi Hills, op. cit.*
15. Choube, S.K. *Hills Politics in North-East India,* Orient Longman, Calcutta 1973, pp. 98-99.
16. Rymbai, R.T. "Relation Between District Councils, Chiefs and Village Government — Role of Traditional Institutions" (Seminar Paper 1987).
17. Pakem, B. "Meghalaya: Some Aspects of Political Development", *op. cit.,* pp. 234–235.

CHAPTER VI

Emerging Political Elites in Jaintia Hills

A strong desire to break away from tradition and move speedily towards modernity is noticed in most of the developing countries. Even if this is the case today, however many of these countries continue to have a nostalgia for some aspects of their own traditions. In many instances, the vision of such traditions is a blurred one. Traditional leadership in these countries is still a force to reckon with. The emergence of politics as the dominant theme of the new nations and the increasing politicisation of individual and his groups in these societies is a fact of great historical, political and sociological significance. But one cannot deny the fact that new pattern of leadership has emerged and this has created a considerable gap between traditional and the new type of leaders.

In our own country, we find that 'the traditional concept of society stratifies India into closed groups with well defined, though circumscribed, roles and relationships.' Thus, historically, the authority structure had largely been ascriptive and feudal. Authority was vested in persons belonging to certain privileged strata of society. Leaders were invariably drawn from among the higher caste groups and in most of the cases leadership was an aspect of the hereditary and family functions. The lower strata of castes and families were totally excluded from occupying positions of political, economic and cultural superiority. Thus according to the traditional concept of society, leadership patterns are unusually rigid and strictly ascriptive.[1] In the case of Jaintia Hills, though the society is by tradition a casteless and classless society, but the traditional pattern of authority and leadership structure was almost the same ascriptive one found elsewhere in

India. Thus, traditional leadership was vested in persons belonging to certain original clan or clans (*Kurs*).

The traditional leaders are 'those who have been operating in the traditional social structure, standing for the old traditional values and institutions and satisfying various traditional needs of the tradition-oriented tribal society . . . All these leaders operate within the traditional social structure and satisfying the religious . . . or secular needs which are traditionally created and are of traditional importance.'[2]

The authors have tried to define the terms 'leader' and 'leadership' in different ways and have given different opinions as regards the understanding of these terms. Hollander opines that 'in general, leader denotes an individual with a status that permits him to exercise influence over certain other individual . . . deriving status from followers who may accord or withdraw it, in an essentially free interchange within a group context. Group consent is therefore a central feature in the leader-follower relationships. . . . '[3] Other definition is that — 'leaders are inseparable from any political network. They have the same importance, purpose and place as the head has in the case of a human body. A political network without a leader is like a rudderless ship. The leaders provide the means to attain the objectives of a political network.'[4] With regard to leadership roles, Hans Nagpaul observes that 'the person who plays a role or function in a situation within the context of the culture to attain a specified goal or goals is perceived as the leader by the members of his group and is given prestige, authority and status which he would not have as a member of the group.'[5]

The traditional leadership in Jaintia Hills fulfils some of the definitions mentioned above. In Jaintia Hills the traditional leaders were that of the *Syiem* or *Raja, Dolois* and Village Headmen, who looked after and maintained the administration of the Syiemship, *Elakas/Illakas* and villages respectively. Before the coming of the British into these hills, the whole of Jaintia Hills formed a single kingdom (Syiemship). The office of the *Syiem* lapsed in 1835 when Jaintia Hills was annexed by the British. Therefore, after the annexation the office of the *Syiem* was abolished and ceased to function. The last Jaintia *Syiem* was given a pension by the British and retired to the British district of Sylhet (now in Bangladesh). The British subsequently declared that the whole area along with few other villages in Khasi Hills to be British Area. But on the other hand, the British retained the offices of *Doloi* and Village Headman and these continue to function till today aiding and assisting the District Council in the district administration.

Though the office of *Syiem* came into existence at the last stage of state formation in ancient Jaintia, but it occupied the apex position in the administrative and leadership hierarchy. Moreover, with regards to internal organisation, the Syiemship was split into twelve units. Each of these units was known as doloiship and this holds good even today. Each of the doloiship was and and is still looked after and nursed by a *Doloi* or Provincial Governor. At the level of village administration, we have a Village Headman (*Waheh Chnong*) who runs and supervises the administration. It was thus during this period (pre-Independence) that the Jaintias had a three-tier system of government — that is, at the top level of administration and leadership we have the *Syiem* or *Raja*; at the zonal stage, below the *Syiem* we have the *Dolois* and at the lowest rung of the ladder of administration, that is at the village level, the Headman.

In Jaintia Hills the authority structure and leadership was patterned in a rigid form and based strictly on ascriptive footings at all the three levels of administration. Succession to the offices was based on a hereditary basis. The Jaintia society being a matrilineal one, hereditary passed from the uncle to the nephew. In case of succession to the office of the Syiem, if it happens that 'the *Syiem* had no more relatives then succession should be decided by means of divination. The principle of divination was actually resorted to in the case of *U Syiem* Ram Singh II (1790–1832) with the help of a local little bird called *Pdia* or parrot giving the divine oracle.'[6] On closer perusal of the right to set up candidates to the office of the *Doloi* it is to be found that only those persons who belong to the original clan(s) have the right to do so. This privilege was granted to them for having originally founded the villages or *Elakas/Illakas*. The general population could not aspire to the elective post of a *Doloi*. Further even from among the original clan or clans, the candidate or candidates for the elective post of a *Doloi* were recruited mostly on ascriptive criteria rather than on grounds of achievements.[7] More or less the same case applied with regards to the Village Headmen.

With the annexation of the plain areas of the Sylhet district (now in Bangladesh) to the Jaintia kingdom through conquest, the *Syiem* ruled over the people both in the hills and the plains. But 'his personal rule prevailed only over the conquered territory of the plain areas. In the hills section, the administration was left entirely to the *Dolois* (Provincial Governors). The only symbol of their allegiance to the *Raja* was an annual tribute of one he-goat from each and every village under their administration. . . . '[8] The *Dolois* continued to pay the same annual tribute to the British authorities at Cherrapunjee instead of taking the tribute as usual during the Rajas' time to Jaintiapur. It was also reported that *Raja* Indra Singh used to receive a few seers of parched rice from most of the villages every year and a few bundles of fire-wood from the places where that wood is found. These articles were expended at the *pujas* at the Rajbari at Jaintiapur. Moreover, every village in turn had to supply the *Raja* with coolies and other servants for cultivating the *Raj* lands and other purposes.[9] This symbol of allegiance was 'rather ceremonial than political — though technically — a tribute system was symbolic of basic power system. The *Raja* was no more than a symbol of unity of the people; and if his activities threatened that unity, the latter would strongly oppose him.'[10] It is therefore evident that though the *Syiem* held the highest office, but it were the people who maintained the highest authority.

The *Dolois* had certain powers and functions delegated to them by the *Syiem*, such as executive, political, judicial and religious. As mentioned earlier, the *Dolois* wielded extensive powers and influence over the hills section of the Syiemship and actually the entire administration was left in their hands.

At the lowest rung of the ladder of administration, we have the Village Headman (*Waheh Chnong*). The Village Headman is the leader of the people within the jurisdiction of the village and is responsible for the maintenance of the administration in various spheres. The presence of the Village Council is also of great help to the Headman. It is in this Council that the whole affairs of village administration, other activities and developments are brought to the notice of all the adult male members of the village as its members. However, it will not be out of place to mention that the highest authority at all the levels of administration rests with the people in general. The authorities, be he the *Syiem*, or *Dolois* or Village Headmen, could not go against the popular opinion of the inhabitants. Those authorities have no dictatorial power over the people because they were selected/elected by the people themselves in order to supervise the administration and not to oppress or suppress them.[11]

An attempt is also made here to examine the emergence of the new type of leaders and the transformation brought about by them in the transitional period in Jaintia Hills. It may be noted that, unlike the past ascriptive traditional set up of the leadership, the new one is based on achievement, measured through acquisition of the elective positions. The new political structure had a serious impact on the traditional political system and administration. It has created a new relationship and roles. There is a sea-change between the traditional and the emerging pattern of roles and leadership.

In the first instance, there was a colonial impact which led to the birth of the new elites in the region. Thus, under the colonial rule, a host of new elites sprang into existence. They formed a new class of their own with the help of their professions like government officials, lawyers, teachers and English educated elites in general. Most of them are urban based. These new educated elites were not lacking behind their counterparts in the plains. Moreover, 'under the colonial rule of the British, the Khasis and Jaintias made fast progress and their society gradually approximated to that of the plains, since the British adopted a policy of 'reclaiming' the hills people to civilization. The result was a series of administrative measures, social and economic reforms in the Khasi-Jaintia Hills whose outcome was the emergence of the middle class.'[12]

The emergence of such political elites and political leaders in Jaintia Hills can also be well seen after India's Independence. This happened because of a new kind of administrative arrangement that was brought about in the hill areas of North-East, that is, the introduction of a democratic political institution under the Sixth Schedule to the Constitution of India, which replaced the British and Indian administrative system for tribal affairs in *Ri Jaintia*.[13] Under the Sixth Schedule to the Constitution of India, District and Regional Councils were introduced in many districts of the hill areas of North East India, including Khasi and

Jaintia Hills. With the introduction of such democratic political institutions in the region, most of the powers and functions of the traditional Chiefs have been taken away and they were put under the control and supervision of the District Council. The traditional leaders are treated only as subordinate officials of the District Council. This had happened because of certain provisions that contained in the Sixth Schedule. For example, under paragraph 3(i)(g) of the said Schedule, the District Council can regulate the appointment or succession of Chiefs and Headman. A specific example may be mentioned here to that of Khasi and Jaintia Hills. The United K-J Hills Autonomous District (Appointment and Succession of Chiefs and Headmen) Act, 1959, made the provisions not only for its authority to appoint the Chiefs and Headmen but even the removal and suspension of the offices by the Executive Committee of the District Council if in its opinion the Chiefs and Headmen violate the terms and conditions of their appointment. Further the Khasi Hills Autonomous District Council in its amendment of the Principal Act on Appointment and Succession of Chiefs and Headmen, 1980, went even to the extent of passing an Act debarring the Chiefs, Deputy Chiefs and Acting Chiefs in taking any part in politics and elections either to the State or District Council. Though this Act does not cover Jaintia Hills, but in practice the *Dolois* and other Chiefs are not permitted to contest the elections and take part in any form in politics. This is another way of control enforced by the District Council over the traditional Chiefs. Thus, under the new constitutional set up, the Chiefs are pushed behind the line. They are to keep themselves content with whatever powers and functions that were left to them by the District Council. Further, under such a precarious situation, frontal leadership in the area or for that matter in the whole state passes into the hands of the emerging elites. The prevailing conditions are therefore more in favour of such elites than the old guards of tradition. Moreover, the District Council having armed with such constitutional powers, have put under it a complete control over the traditional authorities. There are, therefore, drastic effects on the powers and functions of the traditional Chiefs with the coming of the District Council into existence.

"When a society changes from its traditional moorings into a modern society there is a gradual but fundamental change in the style of life of the people and in their outlook on the world. It involves a new orientation in the attitude . . . Modernisation is a total transformation of society, a movement in consciously choosen direction."[14] About this "Choosen direction", there appear two broad major current if we analyse the Jaintia society in the traditional period. One of the currents is an attempt to transform social structure from the ones based on ascriptive to achieving roles; secondly, an attempt at transformation of the traditional political system by making the sanction behind all inhabitants of the area and break away the old practice of allowing concentration of political authority and power only in the hands of the original clans (*Kurs*). This is possible especially after the new democratic set up of parliamentary democracy and the institution of District Council was introduced in the country after Independence. Such practice was not adopted only by the Jaintias, but also by the Khasis and the Garos of Meghalaya and the Mizos of Mizoram. They took advantage of the new political institution of District Council in order to consolidate leadership and bring about political modernisation. What followed was the change over the constitutional path to achieve their political ends and leadership and political identity. Under such an atmosphere, the new elites and new type of leaders emerged in the society. These emerging elites are urban-based and educated. Majority of them are alienated from traditional tribal society and forming their distinct strata in the society in transition.

Thus, "the kingpin of the socio-economic and political determinant is the elite structure in the State. In Meghalaya the traditional elite is giving way to modern elite. While the role of ascriptive leaders like the *Nokmas* and the *Laskars* of Garo Hills, the *Syiems, Lyngdohs, Wahadadars* and the *Sardars* of Khasi Hills, and the *Dolois* of Jaintia Hills has been diminished by their respective District Councils that of modern leaders has increased partly due to their achievement — orientation in the various fields of professions like business, law and teaching. Most of the modern leaders of Meghalaya come mostly from the legal and teaching professions and very few from among the traditional leaders. It is hoped, therefore, that the present political elite of Meghalaya has the capability to cause an interaction between the socio-economic environment and the political institutions prevailing in the State . . . Further, most of the Pre-Independence Leaders from British Areas (of Meghalaya) were western educated, cosmopolitan in outlook and comparatively liberal. They come largely from among the urban elite and continued to be at the helm of affairs even after Independence. The British Areas also provided men who joined hands in the struggle for India's freedom though their contribution could not be adequately appreciated as they were far away from the main theatre of India's struggle for Independence. Presently, political leaders come from every nook and corner of the State irrespective of the fact, whether they come from the erstwhile British Areas or from the erstwhile Khasi States."[15]

After closer examination of the whole process of economic and socio-political development of the Jaintia society in the traditional period, it may be concluded that with the introduction of the new system of administration, the past practice is in the process of disintegration. Though there was no such institutions like in the case of Mizoram, but the fact remains that the new administrative set up helps and gives way and opens an avenue to replace the traditional leaders by that of the representatives of the people elected every five years through adult franchise to the State Legislative Assembly and the District Councils. It is through this present system that educated, intellectual elites, lawyers and businessmen find their way to take up the rein of leadership from the traditional leaders in the form of politics and elections. Unlike the latter, the former are more urban conscious, literate/educated and exposed to the outside world. They no longer remain inside the cocoon of their village jurisdiction and tribal society but are thoroughly exposed to the world outside their own. The new pattern of leadership as it exists today, reflects a transition from individual to collective, from the hereditary to elective and from ascriptive to achievement-oriented. With this, leadership roles have been transformed.

REFERENCES

1. Rangnath, *The Changing Pattern of Rural Leadership in Uttar Pradesh*, Sindhu Publications Ltd., New Delhi, 1974, p. 152.
2. Vidyarthi, L.P. and Rai, R.K. *The Tribal Culture of India*, Concept Publishing Co., Delhi, 1977, p. 233.
3. Hollander, E.P. *Leaders, Groups and Influence*, OJP, 1964, p. 16.
4. Vidyarthi and Rai, *op. cit.*, p. 231.
5. Nagpaul, Hans "Leadership : A Frame of Reference," in, *Leadership in India*, L.P. Vidyarthi, (ed.) Asia Publishing House, London, 1967, p. 60.

6. Pakem B. "State Formation in Ancient Jaintia," Seminar paper on 'Pre-Colonial State Formations in Tribal Regions of East and North-East India', organised by the *Centre for Studies in Social Sciences*, Calcutta, 24–26 July, 1981.
7. Pakem, B. "The Changing Power Structure of the Political Institution of Jaintia Chieftainship," *The Journal of North-East India Council for Social Science Research*, Shillong, Vol. II, No. I, April 1977, p. 2.
8. Pakem, B. "The Socio-Political System of the Jaintia Tribe of Assam; An Analysis of Continuity and Change," in K. Suresh Singh (ed.), *Tribal Situation in India*, Indian Institute of Advanced Study, Simla 1972, p. 353.
9. Allen, W.J. *Report on the Khasi and Jaintia Hills*, 1853; (Reprinted, Govt. Press, Shillong, 1975) p. 4.
10. Pakem, B. *op. cit.* (note 8).
11. Gassah, L.S. "Village Administration in Jaintia Hills — A Comparative Study of Two Villages," *The Journal of NEICSSR*, Shillong, Vol. IV, No. I, April 1980, pp. 11–12.
12. Dutta, P.N. "The Emergence and Role of the Middle Class in the Khasi-Jaintia Hills, 1824–1950," in B. Datta Ray (ed.), *The Emergence and Role of Middle Class in North-East India*, Uppal Publishing House, New Delhi, 1983, pp. 112–113.
13. Pakem, B. *op. cit.* (note-7), p. 3.
14. Aiyar, S.P. *Modernisation of Traditional Society*, MacMillan, Delhi, 1973, p. 4.
15. Pakem, B. "Meghalaya: The Politics of Ethnic Groups," in M.K. Raha and Iar Ali Khan (Eds.) *Polity, Political Process and Social Control in South Asia: The Tribal and Rural Perspectives*, Gyan Publishing House, New Delhi 1993, pp. 168, 170–171.

Bibliography

(Primary Sources)

Annual Report on the Administration of the Khasi and Jaintia Hills (hereafter ARA) for the year 1906-07, No. 802, Shillong 8th May 1907; F.E. Jackson to the Commissioner, Surma Valley and Hill Districts.

ARA for the year 1907–08; No. 484, Shillong, 3 April 1908, Jackson to the Commissioner Surma Valley and Hill District.

ARA for the year ending 31st March 1909; Shillong 12th May 1909; L.O. Clarke to the Commissioner Surma Valley and Hill Districts, Silchar.

ARA for the year 1911-12; No. 3062, Silchar 6th July 1912, Commissioner Surma Valley and Hill Districts to the Chief Secy., Chief Commissioner of Assam.

ARA for the year 1914-15; No. 2106, Shillong 28th May 1915, A.W. Dentith to the Commissioner Surma Valley and Hill Districts.

Census Reports of India, 1961, Vol. III, Part VI, No. 13.

General Administration Report of the Khasi and Jaintia Hills District for the year ending 31st March 1909; No. 867, Shillong 12 May 1909; L.O. Clarke to the Commissioner Surma Valley and Hill Districts.

Home Department Public Consultation A, 13 October 1860, No. 60, Rowlatt to Jenkins, 11 May 1860.

Political Report of the Khasi and Jaintia Hills District for 1890–93; Assam Secretariat Forgn. A. Progs., July 1893, Nos. 22–23; Gray to the Secy. to the Commissioner of Assam, No. 902, Shillong 11 April 1893.

Report of the Commission on the Hill Areas of Assam 1965-66 (Pataskar Commission) Delhi 1966.

Report of the Land Reforms Commission for Khasi Hills, Shillong 1974.

Selection from the Records of the Government of Bengal No. XXXIX, Part I. Papers relating to the disturbances in the Cossyah and Jynteah Hills, Calcutta, 1863; Showers to the Secretary Government of Bengal, 9th June 1862.

Selection from Records, Morton to Major Agnew, 9th July 1862.

Selection from Records, Gordon to Haughton, No. 436, 8th September 1862.

(Secondary Sources)

Ali, Syed Murtaza. *The History of Jaintia, Dacca* 1954.

Allen, W.J. *Report on the Administration of the Cossyah and Jynteah Hill Territory,* 1858, Shillong 1975 (Reprint).

Aitchison, C.U. *Collection of Treaties, Engagements and Sanads Relating to India and Neighbouring Countries,* Vol. XII, Mittal Publications (Reprint) Delhi 1982.

Aiyar, S.P. *Modernisation of Traditional Society,* Macmillan, Delhi 1973.

Bareh, Hamlet. *The History and Culture of the Khasi People,* Shillong 1967.

Bareh, Hamlet. *Khasi Democracy,* Shillong 1964.

Cantlie, Sir Keith. *Notes on Khasi Law* (Ed. and Reprinted by A.S. Khongphai), Shillong 1974.

Choube, S.K. *Hill Politics in North East India,* Orient Longman, Calcutta 1973.

Dutta, P.N. *Impact of the West on the Khasis and Jaintias,* Cosmo Publications, New Delhi 1982.

Dutta, P.N. 'The Emergence and Role of the Middle Class in the Khasi-Jaintia Hills (1824–1950)' in B. Datta-Ray (Ed.) *The Emergence and Role of Middle Class in North East India,* Uppal Publishing House, New Delhi 1983.

Gassah, L.S. 'Village Administration in Jaintia Hills — A Comparative Study of Two Villages', *The Journal of North East India for Social Science Research* (hereafter Journal of NEICSSR), Vol. IV, No. I, April 1980, Shillong.

Gordon, P.R.T., *The Khasis,* Cosmo Publications and (Reprint) New Delhi 1981.

Hadem, Humphrey., 'Suggestions and Objections to the proposed Delimitation of the Seven Legislative Assembly Constituencies for Jaintia Hills, 3rd December 1974 (Mimeograph).

Hollander, E.P., *Leaders, Groups and Influence*, OUP, 1964.

Hunter, W.W., *A Statistical Account of Assam*, Vol. II, (1879), B.R. Publishing Corporation (Reprint) Delhi 1975.

Laloo, S.S., *Ka Behdienkhlam*, (no date).

Lyngdoh, U Homiwell., *Ki Syiem, Khasi bad Synteng*, Shillong 1964.

Mackenzie, A., *The North-East Frontier of India*, Delhi 1979 (Reprint).

Mills, A.J.M., *Report on the Khasi and Jaintia Hills*, 1853, Assam Secretariat Printing office (Reprint) Shillong 1901.

Nagpaul, Hans, 'Leadership: A Frame of Reference' in *Leadership in India*, (Ed.) L.P. Vidyarthi, Asia Publishing House, London 1967.

Pakem, B., 'State Formation in Pre-Colonial Jaintia', *The NEHU Journal of Social Sciences and Humanities* (hereafter NEHU Journal), Nehu Publications, Vol. II, No. 3, July–Sept, 1994 Shillong.

Pakem, B., 'The Changing Power Structure of the Political Institutions of Jaintia Chieftain-Ship', *NEICSSR Journal*, Vol. I, No. I April 1977, Shillong.

Pakem, B., 'The Socio-Political System of the Jaintia Tribe of Assam: An Analysis of Continuity and Change', in *Tribal Situation in India* (Ed.) K.S. Singh, IIAS, Simla 1972.

Pakem, B., 'Meghalaya: Some Aspects of Political Development' in *North East India: A Sociological Study*, (Ed.) S.M. Dubey, Concept Publishing Company, Delhi 1978.

Pakem, B., 'Administration of Justice in Jaintia Hills,' in *Tribal Institutions of Meghalaya* (Ed.) S.K. Chatopadhyaya, Spectrum Publications, Guwahati 1975.

Pakem, B., 'Political Development and Change in North East India', in *Changing North-East India* (Ed.) A.P. Sinha, Gagan Publishers, Ludhiana 1986.

Rangnath: *The Changing Pattern of Rural Leadership in Uttar Pradesh*, Sindhu Publications Ltd., New Delhi 1974.

Rymbai, R.T., 'Relation between District Councils, Chiefs and Village Govt', (Mimeograph), 1987.

Sarma-Roy, B.K., *Ka Histori jong Ka Ri Khasi*, Shillong 1914.

Shadwell, J.B., *Note on the Inhabitants of the Khasi and Jaintia Hills*, 1871, Assam Secretariat Printing office, Shillong.

Trotter, W.F., *Report on the Administration of Jowai for the year ending 31 March 1878*, Calcutta 1878.

Vidyarthi, L.P. and Rai, R.K., *The Tribal Culture of India*, Concept Publishing Co., Delhi 1977.